THE DEAF OF ELVIS
AND THE LAST OF
THE ANGLO INDIANS

Dear friend Alfie,
Best Wishes,
Trevor Taylor
25/7/2020.

Keep playing your
Guitar, Son!

THE DEAF OF ELVIS AND THE LAST OF THE ANGLO INDIANS

AN AUTOBIOGRAPHY BY
TREVOR TAYLOR

TREVOR TAYLOR

Library of Congress Control Number:		2020908180
ISBN:	Hardcover	978-1-9845-9499-0
	Softcover	978-1-9845-9498-3
	eBook	978-1-9845-9497-6

Print information available on the last page.

Rev. date: 06/10/2020

To order additional copies of this book, contact:
Xlibris
800-056-3182
www.Xlibrispublishing.co.uk
Orders@Xlibrispublishing.co.uk
811451

CONTENTS

"Trevor and his wife Zoe"

INTRODUCTION

Anglo Indians emigrated from India when India became independent in 1947.

There was a mass exodus of Anglo Indians who started immigrating to the UK, Australia, New Zealand or the USA and Canada.

It was during 1947 till 1960 that it all happened and was a total culture adjustment living in a foreign land, especially after leaving India with their lives of luxury with servants to do it all and now having to do it all themselves.

On the Anglo Indians' first arrival, if they were dark-skinned, they had to suffer racial remarks, which they never ever had to before. And those who were fair-skinned also suffered racial abuse because of their Anglo Indian accent.

Those Anglo Indian women who were well educated were lucky to get employed as shorthand typists or secretaries, whilst the men with lower education got jobs in the railways, as bus drivers and conductors or the Royal Mail. The well-educated men, especially with fair skin, got better jobs as draughtsmen or other skills.

Anglo Indians finally began to settle and raised families and then related to their children and grandchildren their roots; this next generation of Anglo Indians were not called Anglo Indian because they were born in the UK or wherever and had been born as British. They adapted to that particular country's ways. They also spoke in an English accent and used to make fun of our Anglo Indian accents.

They found it quite difficult to understand their parents' roots, of such a mixture of English, Dutch, Polish, Armenian, Scottish, Welch and Irish.

We are the last of the Anglo Indians of our generation, those who emigrated during 1947 till 1960.

May our children and great-grandchildren live on to tell the world of the famous 'Anglo Indians'.

I was in two minds about leaving India for good because after so many difficult years, I felt that I was living the life of a king in comfort of every kind. I was getting the itch to leave India as I was beginning to realise that Anglo Indians did not really fit in India any longer. The English side of my birth was calling me to England. How could I leave the place where I was born and ate the salt of the land of Mother India? I was in turmoil and totally confused.

To all my readers, I have written this book to help anyone suffering from deafness or hearing loss cope with it.

To my beautiful wife, Zoe, and my dear mum, Eva Mona, who sadly passed away on Christmas Day 2010.

As well as my father, Kevin George, who passed away in Bombay in 1954 and my sister, Jean, who died a teenager at 16 years old in Bombay in 1952.

My autobiography is inspired by many of my close Anglo Indian friends and family, especially my wife, Zoe, and my three kids – my eldest son, Rudy, and my two daughters Michelle and Nicky – my seven grandkids – Kyle, Jordan, Tegan, Taylor Scott, Ryan Singleton, Max and Jake Campbell – as well as my brothers Edward and Jimmy and sisters Joyce and Maureen. Not forgetting my great-granddaughter Lily Elizabeth Taylor.

ACKNOWLEDGMENTS

I have written this book for all Elvis fans throughout the world and for the millions of followers. A special thanks to Jeffery Chapman, my nephew, who gave me an idea of the book's title, and Sydney Ledlie, who also contributed to some corrections in my book.

A special Thanks to my grandson Max Campbell for his artwork and design, and his Mother Niki (my daughter) for her excellent photography.

From left to right: Jean my sister, myself aged three,
My Bro Eddie & Elder Sister Joyce.

CHAPTER 1

THE DEAF OF ELVIS

Why 'The Deaf of Elvis'? A very good question. Later on in my story, you will understand why I am deaf and what the connection has to do with Elvis and how I grew to like and sing in the Elvis Presley style.

I was born with defective ears, and from the age of about 2, I used to suffer from earaches, which were very painful. My mum in those days used to put peroxide in my ears to make them fizz to remove the excess wax build-up, but only in my adult years did I discover that peroxide was dangerous for the ears as it sort of ate into the eardrums and perforated them. Unfortunately, that was the treatment in the old days, and doctors don't allow it now. I used to suffer a lot of pain and was constantly being rushed to the doctors as my mum tried her best to comfort me, with not much success.

I was born in Nagpur, India, on 5 October 1940. My dad worked on the GIP railways in Nagpur. My mum and dad moved to Bombay around about 1942, where we stayed with my uncle Peter Rocque at Byculla, Bombay, for a while until my uncle fixed us up to stay at 44/48 Fort Street Dehudusty Building on a third-floor flat, where we lived for many years until we all left for the UK.

India was still under the British rule of King George VI, and India was fighting for independence under Mahatma Gandhi and Pundit Nehru. There were lots of riots with Hindus and Muslims killing each other, and the British rulers had to control these riots, which gradually got out of control. Then finally, the British sent Lord Mountbatten to India to sort out the Indian independence, which was finally agreed on 15 August 1947.

India was now independent and started to get rid of the British rulers who had so many years of good life in India. Lord Mountbatten and his family were very sad to leave India as he had a very close relationship and a close friend with Pundit Nehru, the prime minister of India.

There was a mass exodus of British leaving India, along with the Anglo Indians of British decent with their British passports. Anglo Indians basically felt unwanted, and if we wanted to still stay in India. we were to accept Indian citizenship with an Indian passport.

Anglo Indians were brought up and lived all our lives like the British, went to English schools, lived and dressed in Western clothes and spoke only English as our mother tongue. All throughout our lives, we lived in British or American style, and although we had Indian friends at school, we were taught in English as our first language, and Hindustani was our second language. Anglo Indians spoke very basic Hindi to get by with our Indian servants, as did the British whilst living in India. Anglo Indians were only too glad to move out of India now that it was independent and everything was now under Indian rules, so Anglos decided to immigrate to the Western world, where we would fit in better. This started a mass exodus of Anglo Indians leaving for the UK, Australia, America and Canada.

What Is an Anglo Indian?

According to the *Penguin English Dictionary*, an Anglo Indian is a British person who lived for a long time in India, especially during the time when India was part of the British Empire or a Eurasian of mixed British and Indian birth or descent or relating to or denoting relations between British and India, especially during the period when India was a British colony or relating to or denoting Anglo Indians.

My name is Trevor Hugh Anthony Taylor. (Very English-sounding, isn't it?) Well, how could I be half Indian with a name like THAT? They are my initials (Trevor Hugh Anthony Taylor), and come to think of it, being born in India with Anglo Indian parents, how did I get such an English name?

Well, on my father's side, I was of Irish ancestry, and my mother's side was of Turkish decent. Most Anglos are Scottish/Indian or Welsh/Indian, Dutch/Indian, Portuguese/Indian or Armenian/Indian.

Some of the Anglo Indians were given up for adoption to orphanages as the British father responsible for the child had either gone back to England or did not want to father the child as he was already married in England, or it was a shame that he had an affair with an Indian woman. If a British army officer came with his English wife to stay in India and she was having an affair with an Indian, because of the shame and disgrace it would cause, she would probably abort or give the child up for adoption to an orphanage, which was usually Dr Bernados in Kalimpong, India.

During the British Raj in India, British officers and top government officials who were sent out to India were given lavish homes, which they built in British styles, and were also given servants such as *kansamas* (cooks) and an *aayah* (a nanny or general house servant), a *jamadhar* (a sweeper), a *maali* (a gardener), a *methrani* (a toilet cleaner) and a 'boy' to run errands and open the doors for visitors, serve the food and drinks, empty the ashtrays and fetch fresh glasses and ice for drinks on the verandas. They also had *punkawallahs* (a person to fan them with large fans made of sisal and coir suspended from the ceiling down to floor to keep them cool). The punkawallahs sprinkled the *punkas* and floors with cool water to keep away the heat and the dust.

Most of the top-ranking British officers without their wives in India, as they were back home in England, were paid an extra allowance to take an Indian wife. Sometimes they also had an affair with the aayah, thus resulting in the making of an ANGLO INDIAN child. Quite fascinating, wasn't it? Yes, Anglos intermarried, increased and multiplied as time went on. We took the British names, and sometimes even the illegitimate child of the aayah was given English, Scottish, Irish or Welsh names. The British Lords and Ladies had it made in India, moving up to the hill stations during the hot summer months to cooler places such as Nanital, Ooti, Bangalore, etc. with all the trimmings of full staff of servants, ayahs, kansamas, etc.

The Gateway of India (Top photo) Fort Area, Bombay.

Victoria Terminus Station, Bombay (We lived behind it)

During Queen Victoria's time, countless Victorian-styled buildings and infrastructures were built. One of the many typical Victorian structures was the Victoria Terminus Railway Station, which was a hop step and a jump from where I had lived for the last eighteen years or so in old Bombay at Fort Street near Red Gate, Alexandra Docks, near the Rex Cinema at Dehudusty Building.

Mostly all the great municipal buildings, law courts, dockyards, cinemas and names of streets and roads were under British names, such as Flora Fountain, the GPO building, Ballard Pier, Colaba Causeway, Frere Road, Byculla, and the famous Berkeley Building, which was an Anglo Indian railway quarters, as most of all the Anglos worked on the railways.

The British in India employed the Anglos as negotiators to the Indian workers because the Anglos spoke Hindi as well as English and got the work done. We spoke only English at home and went to English-speaking schools and, of course, spoke Hindustani as a second language, which we picked up from our servants or the locals. We spoke in Pigeon Hindi, which got us by and kept the British happy.

The schools, colleges and convents were of a very high standard. The Oxford and Cambridge examination papers were from England, and those educated in these schools were taught by English teachers or priests and nuns. On the other hand, there were matriculation class of schools, which were also taught in English but had Indian-, Goan- or Spanish-speaking teachers who had vernacular accents, and so compared with the Cambridge and Oxford students, the matric school Boys and girls spoke with a vernacular accent.

The typical not-so-well-spoken Anglo Indian way of expressing themselves were words such as 'What men, what to tell you men', 'Oh, you buggar', 'Go and bugger off' and 'What you talking men, damn bloody fool'. When old pals met, they would greet each other as 'Hey you, bugger' or 'Trevor, you bugger, where have you been? Dammit'. It was all very friendly, and no one took any offence.

In 1944, there was a huge explosion on the docks of Bombay. I was told Bombay was a natural harbour which was totally destroyed by this huge explosion caused by ships carrying ammunition. The fire then caused a chain reaction to all the ships that were docked as they exploded.

My dad was then working on the docks as a medical doctor and had his own sort of caravan cabin as a makeshift quarters to treat injured or sick dock workers. We used to visit him there, and he was always very pleased to see us. Dad came out after the explosion with his ears bleeding to rescue us from the dangers of the aftermath of the explosion. I was about 4 years old and remember sitting on the easy chair and my mum saying, 'Tea is ready', as she was churning the old metal teapot. I will never forget that sound of the old metal teapot when all of a sudden, there was BANG, BOOM, BANG, BOOM, BOOM, BOOM, the loudest I ever heard. There was panic everywhere with my mum gathering us all under her wings and taking whatever she could. She asked us to hurry up and get the hell out of our apartment as the whole place was shaking, being so close to the docks. It was like an earthquake. I thought it was the end of the world.

We were taken to the League of Mercy a few miles away in Byculla, as I don't remember very much after that. It must have been the massive shock, and I was told later on by my brothers and sisters that before leaving for the ambulance to take us away as arranged by our dad, I was kneeling and praying in front of Our Sacred Heart picture we had on the wall and saying, 'Please, God, don't let anything happen to our house.' That I think was the start of my ears going from bad to worse. Mum used to take me to the J. J. Hospital for the treatment of my ears, which used to discharge, and my hearing was just starting to deteriorate.

To conclude my theory of 'The Deaf of Elvis', I will explain later on the influence Elvis had on me, how I started to sing like him, although I was at the time partially deaf.

Just to mention the name Elvis – there's no need to mention Presley – and everyone knows who you are on about, especially if you are an Anglo Indian, as the one and only 'ELVIS' is, was and always will be a household name to us Anglos as we liked to be called or AIs in short.

Myself on top row, far right at St.Xavier's High School, Bombay in 1956

CHAPTER 2

SCHOOL DAYS

I was educated at St Xavier's High School, Bombay, at Dhobi Talau, near Crawford Market and the famous Metro Cinema. We had mostly wealthy Indian students who were Parsi, Hindus, Goans or Muslim boys, and our teachers were either Spanish priests of the Jesuit order or Goan and some Anglo Indian teachers as well. Owing to our British upbringing at home, Anglos spoke English a little better than the Indian boys because their mother tongue was not English. So mixing with Indian boys, we Anglos developed a peculiar accent compared with those educated at the posh schools of Oxford and Cambridge, who spoke 'ever so well indeed'.

I was a very clever lad at St Xavier's and topped the class in my younger years. Then as the years went by and I got to the 1Xth standard, I got mixed up with bad company and started 'bunking off' with my brother Jimmy and a few other Anglo boys who didn't go to school at all as their parents could not afford to send them to school. Some were just plain lazy and did not want to work hard and opted for the 'cushy' way of life and were either alcoholics or gamblers. Some even became pimps and prostitutes.

The area where I lived was near Red Gate Alexandra Docks, where we got a lot of 'shippies' (sailors) as we used to call them. The Brits were called Tommies and the Americans Yanks, or even Greek, Norwegian and Dutch ships also docked there, so you can imagine what it was like living *On the Waterfront*. It reminded me of the movie, and I was a young delinquent like Marlon Brando – tough, mean and moody, not much time to be bothered going to school, which wasn't cool. We stole comic books and flogged them to the rich Indian boys at school who paid us well enough so that when we bunked school, we could afford to go to all the latest English movies or even sometimes the Hindi movies, now called Bollywood movies. We were surrounded with prostitutes to the left and right sides of where we lived, who used to look out for the sailors coming out of the docks, along with their pimps looking out to make a quick buck.

L/R, me, Heather Pascoe, Sister Joyce, Sydney Fraser
Linda Downs, Eddie with baby Latha.

Myself centre with guitar sideways left of mic with shoelace
bow, at Taj Hotel Bombay, makings of a Bollywood Star.

CHAPTER 3

THE BOLLYWOOD STAR

Speaking of 'Bollywood movies', I was a Bollywood 'extra' in an Indian movie called *Love Marriage* in the year 1957, with the Indian 'Gregory Peck' actor named Dev Anand. My brother Eddie and a few other Anglo boys and myself went to the Andheri's film studios in Bombay and did a five-day shoot and were paid quite handsomely. The scene we took part in was at a so-called nightclub; we had to mime to rock and roll music, with me as a young Elvis and doing my Elvis moves and a load of Anglo 'jivers' strutting their stuff in the five-minute scene with my brother Eddie on drums, my mate Colin Downs on 'maracas' and the Indian director Subbodh Mukerjee going crazy with my actions and stuff. He was quite taken in by me as I was quite bold. He told me that I had the makings of becoming a true Bollywood star as I was quite bold and not camera shy and that if I were to learn to speak Hindi properly, he would offer me 'speaking' roles that would make me into a real 'Bollywood Star', but I did not take the offer as I was only 17 years of age and a real Bombay 'goonda' (loafer).

As I said earlier, living on the waterfront didn't help. It was not a very decent area, full of pimps and whores, and when I was about 12 or 14, I started smoking and had a mate, Maurice, who lived with his sister. She used to give her brother Maurice and me money to buy 'kites' or go to the movies.

THE KITE RUNNERS

Now kite flying was very popular in Bombay, and like the movie *The Kite Runner*, it was just like that, where they used to have kite flying competitions and huge bets on whose kites would win the kite fight.

The string known as *maanja* is the stronger twine covered with 'powdered glass', which we made. The maanja was a sun-dried string, which rolled onto a *feerki* (a wooden reel about a foot wide and handles on either ends to roll up the maanja). Whilst the main kite fighter controlled the path of the kite's flight, the maanja guy controlled the 'feerki'.

It was not only flying for fun. The hobby was quite expensive as some of the kites were in very beautiful colours, shapes and sizes, and of course, the 'maanja' quality counted a lot as well. The men used to have huge bets on which kite would win, and then there were the kite runners who took enormous risks running after the kite that lost the fight.

They would chase the lost kite over rooftops, trees and through traffic or railway lines, anything to capture the prized kite that lost the fight as it was worth quite a good bit of rupees. The 'Azad Maidaan', which compared with a huge 'common' in England, was where the big kite fights would take place. We had huge crowds on either ends of the 'maaidan'. One lot of guys would have a kite fight, and of course, big money bets were laid on who would be the kite champ of that particular year. Kite flying was quite a big business in Bombay, and the professional kite makers did very well with their exquisite brands of kites and maanjas of different strengths and colours. Sorry to say, a few deaths occurred with the kite runners. There were some serious accidents or even fights among the runners to be the first to catch the 'lost prized kite'.

Yes, I loved my kite flying. We used to get up on my terrace on the top of my third-floor building and spend a lot of time up there. My mum also was a keen kite flyer and used to teach us how to fly the kites when we were little. She showed us how to make our own kites and maanja and feerkis. Those were the days, my friend. I still dream of those days when we were young and innocent with kite flying and didn't think of the dangers and risks we went through.

Yes, those were the days to last me a lifetime – good old Bombay, the kites, the betting and the atmosphere of the humid Bombay air, the heat and the dust – never to be forgotten.

GILLI DANDA

Gilli Danda was a sort of game where we sliced a piece of wood about three inches long and tapered the ends of the rounded wood So when you hit one end of the tapered piece with a stick about twelve inches long, the tapered bit would bounce up, and the skill was to hit the tapered bit as hard as possible. The winner was the one who hit the gilli further. It was a simple game that gave us a lot of fun.

Then we also played the poor man's cricket, where we drew stumps on a wall and made our bats out of any spare pieces of wood we could find. We used tennis balls to bowl with in the hot burning sun, which we enjoyed after with a nice cold glass of water or lassie or sugarcane juice.

CHAPTER 4

THE CARUSO!

I was always a Caruso as a little boy as I used to sing along with my parents' gramophone player to old Johnny Ray records and old songs my dad used to sing when he was tipsy. He was of Irish decent and used to sing songs like 'Danny Boy' and 'I'll Take You Home Again Kathleen', and my little sister also used to sing as well and did a song called 'My Happiness'.

I used to play with an old shoebox and pretend it was a gramophone and made paper discs to look like records, which was the old 78s in the early 1940s, and my mum and dad used to sing the old Second World War songs, which I picked up as well.

My uncle who lived at Byculla, a bus or tram ride away from where I lived in Fort Street near the GPO building, so we used to visit my uncle Peter Rocque, who was quite well off. He owned the hotel he lived in with lots of servants. There was plenty of booze and wild parties, and of course, my dad and mum were there too. My dad and his friends would all be merry and tipsy and start the singing and dancing, and then the star of the show would be either my young sister or me, to give a special show and sing as well as we could, after which my uncle would pay us handsomely with some pocket money.

My uncle Peter knew I had a bit of temper, and to try me out, he said to me that he defied me to run and poke a dagger into his fat gut. He was laughing and teasing me that I didn't have the guts to do it, and then to his surprise, I took the dagger and took a long run straight for his gut, and then he really got scared and told me to stop and gave me a big hug and a kiss and some more pocket money. That was my uncle Peter Rocque.

The Choir Boy

As I was a bit of a Caruso, I was picked for the school choir after an audition and therefore selected to sing in the St Xavier's choir. The audition was to sing in tune, the 'do re mi fa sol la si do. Some of the others were eliminated, and when my turn came, I sailed through and was then selected for the choir. I was elated.

The choirmaster was a Spanish priest who spoke Pigeon English but was an angelic man of God, the kindest and most patient man who guided and conducted the choir and me in the most expressive manner I've ever known.

It was as if an angel of God was guiding us with his wings and inspiring the choir and me to sing with special emotion and feelings. It was the best experience that happened to me as a choir boy, being selected to sing with the soprano's section of the choir. Our choir consisted of alto boys' voices and adult men tenor and bass voices and also a brass section with trumpets, flutes and violins. We had a massive sound, and I was in heaven.

After being in the choir for a few weeks, I was asked if I would like the opportunity to sing as a soloist as the previous soloist, Jocquim, was struggling to sing the solos. His voice was starting to break, and wow, we did; I jump at the chance. I used to envy Jocquim and wondered when I could be soloist. The choirmaster and the chief organist, Mr Paul Frank, started to coach me as soloist, and there I was, 9 or 10 years old, and finally, my dream of being the soloist came true.

One of the treasured moments of my choir boy days was the Christmas midnight Mass at St Xavier's sports ground. It was held in the open air, and it was a bit of a chilly night, but there I was. At that young age, I had to sing the solo part of 'Adeste Fidelis' in Latin and with this massive choir of the full orchestra of violins, trumpets, boys of altos and sopranos and men of bass and tenors. I had to take the lead, and boy, was I nervous, but I knew I had to do it, took a deep breath and sang the opening line: 'Adeste fidelis, regum triumph fantes, venite venite in Bethelem.' The rest of the choir and orchestra came in with a thunderous 'Natum vidite, regum angelorum', and then me alone: 'Venite adoremus, venite adoremus' and then 'venite adoremus' with the rest of the choir. I felt my hair stand and had goose pimples all over. I was in heaven, this little 10-year-old from the docklands of Bombay. I was so proud, and so were my family. I was in my Lord Jesus's arms and guided by his angels.

CHAPTER 5

THE ALTAR BOY

Father Comez, another Spanish priest of the Jesuit order who was deaf, used an old type of hearing aid device which was shaped a bit like a trumpet. It had a metal tube that went into his ear passage, and it folded up in a telescopic manner to a bowl of which you had to speak into. He used to have it looped up to the belt of his Cossack, and if you spoke to him, he would whip it out and extend the bit into his ear. He was a very jolly priest and encouraged me to be an altar boy. Then five o'clock in the morning, I was there every day, prompt, and Father Comez, who used to call me Prince Trevor, would be waiting for me to say the Mass, all in Latin, of course, half of which today I can just about remember.

Here I was this innocent altar boy all dressed up in red-and-white slipover vestments, which I also wore as the choir boy. Then how did I suddenly become this juvenile delinquent, smoking, drinking, bunking school, stealing, telling lies, mixing with bad company, etc.? I guess I could put it down to living in the ghettos of Bombay, with its pimps and whores and cheap 'country liquor', which was an illegal booze distilled and sold very cheaply. Bombay was a dry area where alcohol was prohibited, compared with places like Delhi and the places up north, where booze was flowing freely with no restrictions. So in Bombay, it was big business for those in the booze market. They (some of the smart-suited, Chicago-styled gangsters who were Anglos) are very sharp and well spoken, used to do a deal with the shippies as we used to call them, the Yanks or Limeys (English) or Greek or Italian or Norwegian seamen. We traded them the genuine 'Johnny Walker', black labels, which fetched big money from the rich Indians who paid handsomely for the good stuff. This good stuff was then opened by the skilled booze traders and diluted so as to make one bottle into two, and the rich Indians were none the wiser whilst the smart Anglo racketeer made his quick buck.

The Blue Dens

Beside the booze racket was the dope racket selling 'marijuana' and 'Ganga' to 'shippies', who also paid very well as it was illegal stuff in their countries.

The 'Blue Dens' as we used to call them were holes in walls. In a makeshift dope, den was covered with just a sheet of dirty cotton or a corrugated tin roof hidden and away from the cops. The dope or 'blues' trader would make you welcome and invite you in for some Ganga on the 'chillum', which was a cone-shaped clay pipe usually black or brown through the continuous smoking. A piece of moistened rag was at the bottom of the chillum to keep it cool. The cone was filled with a pre-burnt Ganga ball and mixed with cigarette tobacco and was light from the top of the cone. In a sucking motion you drew the dope smoke into your lungs and held it there for a few seconds and let it out real slow to really get the high.

Yes, old Bombay in the 1940s and 1950s was really rockin' and rollin'. It was a bit like Chicago in the 1920s or the Bronx of New York, filled with all sorts places of vice such as the billiard saloon, where there were heavy bets by the snooker players, and when I was 10 to 12 years of age, my friends and I would hang about and kill time watching the snooker games. Often, we were told off for messing about and told to leave. Snooker and billiards were very popular with the top Anglo snooker 'hustlers', who would play against rich Indian players. They would throw a few games and let the Indian think he was a really top player and then win a few to make it look good, and finally, after a few hours of hustling, the Indian would finally give in and buy us all a good drink.

Then there was also the Mahalakshmi Race Course, and some of the well-off Anglo hustlers would go off to the horse races and either win a fortune or lose by a 'photo finish'.

The Saata Numbers

Betting on the *saata* numbers was another gambling craze in Bombay. This was betting on the opening and closing figures of the New York cotton market, the last two digits of when the New York market's opening and closing figures. We would put our bets with the cycle hire shop owner. You could bet on either the opening figure or bet on both the opening and closing figures for a double amount in your stake.

I remember the time when a friend we knew did hypnotism. This friend whom we used to call Velu was a South Indian and was in the Indian navy and studying law. He claimed he knew hypnotism, so as a joke, we took him up on his offer. He then started to hypnotise me. I was about 12 years old, and at first, my mates and my brother Jim were all giggling about and making fun of the whole idea, but then suddenly, to my surprise, I started to feel a bit sleepy. I could hear his voice still speaking to me whilst I was in a trance, and he asked me what I could see in my semi dream.

I said I could see a man throwing a rope, and it formed the figure 3, and then he asked me what else the man was doing, and I said the man threw the rope again and formed the figure 4. Then he clicked his fingers to wake me up and asked if I remembered the dream, and I said yes, so he then said to me that the two figures that I saw in my dream were 3 and 4, and that were the two figures to bet as a double, i.e. '34', to bet as a double in open to close.

We were all very excited and couldn't wait to place our bets and prove if the hypnotist Velu was right. So off we all went to the cycle man to place our bets, and to make matters even better, we told all our other Anglo friends to bet on these numbers. The other Anglo guys had a lot more money than us lads, who were only small fry and couldn't afford a big bet. So when the results finally came up in the next morning's papers, we couldn't wait to see the results of the New York cotton market opening and closing figures, and guess what. 'We all made a killing.' We were all mega rich and how I'd wished we had more rupees to bet unlike all the other Anglos who had money to burn. They asked me when the next time for another hypnotism session was. It never happened again; it was just the one off. The cycle man wasn't too happy. He used to hide all the betting slips illegally underneath a creaky staircase of the three-storey building where we lived. That is the story of the cycle man and the SAATA numbers.

My Dad in his army uniform with Mum

My beautiful mum in her WAACI uniform

my Dad in Army Uniform

My Dad Kevin

My Beloved Sister died age just 16

Jean (second eldest) in Bombay

My Eldest sister Joyce aged 18

CHAPTER 6

THE TAYLOR FAMILY

My mother, Eva Mona – God bless her soul – died at the ripe old age of 100 in England. My father, Kevin George, died at the age of 52 in Bombay in 1954 when I was 14 years old. My sisters Joyce and Jean and my brother Edward were older than me; I was the fourth child. Then I had a brother James and a sister Maureen, who were younger than me, so all we six kids lived in this third-storey flat in Dehudusty Building, 44/48 Fort Street, Bombay, up until 1960, when I immigrated to the UK. Before the move to England, we were all one big happy family.

My mum would teach us how to fly kites from our veranda as she was a bit of a tomboy, and my dad didn't much care about kites and was more interested in his booze. I loved my dad, and he was very fond of me and used to nickname me 'Travvandrum' as I was quite chubby, and he used to pinch my cheeks. I was quite fair in complexion and had sort of gingery hair I had inherited from my dad. He was very handsome and white-skinned with green eyes and looked a bit like the actor Robert Taylor, and because of his good looks and being a white Anglo, he passed off as an Englishman. He got offered all the best jobs by the British, but sorry to say, because of his excessive boozing, he had lost most of them. The times when he was seldom sober, he was the loveliest dad in the world and would give us heaps of pocket money but didn't give my mum much towards the housekeeping.

My mum was not a very happy mum as she had to struggle to bring us up and to feed, clothe and educate us all. She had to take up a job with the WACCI'S with the British headquarters in Bombay. During the 1940s, she was a code breaker with the war office and was a very proud and intelligent woman and held the 'fort' and would not give up on us kids. She then applied for assistance from the Anglo Indian chairman Mr Brown or Budda Brown as he was known, who then offered my mum funds from the AI Association for our schooling and general stuff required to run the house. Mr Budda Brown admired her for her courage as she held her head up, was always smartly dressed and was highly respected in our neighbourhood as they all knew about my dad and his boozing ways.

The local men or boys used to carry him up three flights of stairs and say they had found Taylor Sahib drunk and couldn't leave him on the streets. My poor mum had to put up with my drunken dad for years and years until the day he finally died due to a burning fag end he slept with, when well sozzled and burnt himself, with the smouldering blanket that covered him. I will never ever forget it. He did get a bit better, and we thought he was going to recover as he asked us to bring him his favourite 'Charminar' cigarettes. He looked like he was going to recover, all fresh in the face and signs of life again, but very sadly, he went down again and finally passed away. His burns were first degree, and plus with all that alcohol in his system, he didn't stand a chance.

I don't remember much after his death as I think I was in a state of shock and do not remember his funeral as well. The only thing that stuck in my mind was the hospital (St George's). He was in a room full of flowers, and to this day, the smell of all those flowers makes me feel sick and did not want to attend any more funerals after that. Then to add to my father's death, I also had the memory of my sister Jean who died two years prior to my dad, so I was still suffering from the shock of my sister Jean. She was the second eldest and died at the tender age of 16. She was so full of life and pretty as my mum. She and my sister Joyce (the eldest) were forced to leave school early to support all of us because there was no income from my dad at all. My two sisters Joyce and Jean went to work at an earlier age than required. My sister Joyce loved reading novels and loved to play with my earlobes as I was quite cute and chubby. She used to pay me to play with my ears with one hand whilst the other hand she used to twirl her hair round and round in circles. She was a very loving and caring sister.

Jean was also a gem and Bombay's jive champ with her jive partner and boyfriend, Dougie Quigley. My sis was only 16, but a real-hot jiver, and she and Dougie won a few jive competitions. She was so full of life and the apple of my mum's eye. I learnt to jive myself from Dougie and Jean, which didn't last too long because as I was picking up the basics of the jive, my sis Jean passed away in a horrible accident at the Strand Cinema, Colaba, Bombay. She and Dougie had a lovers' tiff during the movie; Dougie said she threatened to jump over the balcony at the Strand Cinema out on to the foyer. He said he tried to stop her jumping over but was too late. She landed about two storeys down, causing a nine-inch gash on her head. She was unconscious for nine days and never recovered. To this day, we will never hear her side of what really happened. My mum and all of us were devastated, and my mum was in a daze for months and months after that, and so was my drunken dad. His drinking just got worse, and that was why he died two years later.

Whilst my dad was alive and boozing well, he gave my mum no money to manage as he drank it all, and they used to have countless rows about it, but she never abandoned him or us and held her head up high. When my youngest sis Maureen was born in 1943, there was no milk to feed her properly, and my mum used to send my big sis Joyce to look for my dad in all the booze joints to ask him for some money for baby's milk and to feed us. We could not afford servants, and my mum did all the cooking and housework and went to work as well. We didn't know where our next meal was coming from. My mum had a credit bill with the butchers at Crawford Market, Bombay, and the butchers and other shop owners had so much respect for my mum as no matter what, she always paid her bills. Even if it was a bit late, they would understand.

My mum had to bluff the ages of Joyce and Jean to get them employment in Glaxo Laboratories at Worli, Bombay. Joyce and Jean gave all their wages to my mum, but they were only teenagers and longed for the things teenage girls needed such as plastic shoes that were the fashion in the 1940s, but they deprived themselves and gave the whole wage packet to my mum to clothe, educate and feed us all. My two sisters were like Mother Teresa – God bless them – as they looked after all of us. Joyce was very pretty and resembled Rita Hayworth, and all the guys fancied her. She was extra generous to us as she used to come back after a day's work and gave us money for sweets, etc.

Mum used to take us for Sunday Mass at Woodhouse Church on Sundays and afterwards for a treat to a posh restaurant for cakes and tea. When she was broke and couldn't afford to take us again, we would ask why, and she would joke and say you'll get 'kicks and tea' instead. Mum was brilliant and made sure we had new clothes and shoes for Christmas or our birthdays, and I remember her asking me what would I fancy eating on my birthday, and I would say 'an omelette'. Eggs were very scarce in our household, so we were happy with whatever we were given. Mum used to take us every year in the month of September to the 'Bandra Fair', which was the feast of Our Lady the Mother of Jesus, so we used to save up all our pocket money in an old cigarette tin and spend it on all sorts at the fair and light candles for the sick and sufferings. It was a fantastic day out for us, and I will never forget the eighth of September and the Bandra Fair, which was a train's journey from Fort area to Bandra.

Dehudusty Building, we lived on the 3rd floor flat.

Jimmy, Eddie (my bros) & baby sister Maureen
and I in Bandra Fare days

CHAPTER 7

DEHDUSTY BUILDING

Dehdusty Building, where we lived on the third floor, was quite a big flat for us six kids and my mum and dad. We had the landlord, Mr Dehdusty, living on the right side of us, and to the left, we had Hindu neighbours. We two families shared the one toilet, which was down the corridor about twelve yards away, and indoors, we had our own kitchen/diner and a 'Mori', which is the Indian term for a wash and bathing area. It had a huge drum full of water, which we used to pour into *baltis* (buckets) to wash or bathe. We had a tap to fill the drum from 6 p.m. to 10 p.m. daily as there were water restrictions in the whole of Bombay. We were lucky to have a tap to fill our water as we were more fortunate than the other neighbours who lived opposite us as they had to go down three flights of stairs to get their water from the roadside water supply after 6 p.m.

We were also fortunate to have a veranda overlooking the main road as we used to watch all the actions down below. When it was very hot, we used to lay a rug on the cool tiled floor and sleep there some nights. When it was very hot and we couldn't sleep, we would hear and see the huge crowds coming out of the late night movie around midnight and see them all talking aloud and smoking their *beedies* (a poor man's cigar). It had this distinctive smell, somewhat like a cigar but were much smaller and cheaper, of course, not forgetting the *paan*, which went along with the beedies. The paan was beetle nut wrapped in the paan leaf with a red sweet and bitter paste, which was chewing and sucking in the juices for digestion. Sometimes the paan had a bit of dope in it to relax you. The Indians who were addicted to it used to spit out the extra red juices they couldn't swallow. We used to see this red stuff all over the pavements, walls and streets. The guy who used to sell the paan was called the Paan Beedie Wallah.

I used to sleep sharing a bed with my brother, and my mum slept alongside so she could play with my hair and put me off to sleep. When I was about the age of 12 or 14 and started to mature, one night I got an urge to go to the toilet. When I finished with the toilet, I was confronted by my neighbour's stepdaughter.

Myself aged 14 year (Stud)

MY FIRST KISS

She was a very attractive young Indian girl about the same age as me but well matured for her age and well developed, with big busts and a healthy figure on her. She didn't speak English at all, and I struggled with the little Hindi I knew, so she asked me how I was feeling and said that she liked me and gave me the feeling that she fancied me. So I went all hot and sweaty and started to get excited down below, and before I knew it, she got hold of me and started to kiss me. This was the first time I was ever kissed by a girl on my lips. The feeling was ecstatic, and before I knew what was happening, she put her tongue into my mouth and started to twirl her tongue around and round my tongue. Now I was really worked up. I was in seventh heaven. We parted suddenly with a big smile to each other, and I hurried back to my bed.

My mum was disturbed when I returned and asked me if I was OK. I said yes very nervously, and she went to stroke my hair as usual to put me off to sleep again and discovered I was hot and sweaty. She asked me if I was feeling well and said, 'I think you have a temperature.' I said in a stammer, 'No, no, I'm feeling great, I mean, I'm O-O-OK', and pushed her hand away in embarrassment. I didn't know if she knew or understood what I was going through or what I'd just experienced for the very first time. I finally fell off to sleep.

Those amorous meetings with my neighbour's stepdaughter were my first, and I started to feel that I was a real stud, although I didn't really experience any sex until I met Jane Moore, who was an Anglo Indian girl about the same age as me or a bit younger. She was very fair and pretty and still in school. On her holidays from the convent where she was a boarder, she would return after her holiday period was finished. We met the first time on the first floor of our building where her mother, Patsy, was renting a flat temporarily till she moved to a flat in Byculla.

Jane was about 13 or 14 and had to go back to boarding school, but before she moved to Byculla, whilst staying at Hotel Friends on the first floor of our building, which was next door to our friend Velu (who was the guy who hypnotised me), I used to see Jane at this flat she was sharing with her mum. Then she'd go back to her convent, and when she later returned to the Byculla flat, I would visit her there. I was not really serious about Jane, and of course, after my first lesson in kissing from my Indian neighbour, I didn't need much more coaching from Jane as she and I were just a temporary thing. All the while, my Indian neighbour knew I was seeing Jane, and seeing less of her, she started getting jealous of Jane and told me that I wasn't interested in her because I had found someone who was fairer-skinned than her, 'wo goree me khali' as she said to me in Hindi, which meant that she was black and Jane was white. I was now torn between two lovers and felt quite proud of myself.

Whilst staying at Dehdusty Building, my brother Jim and I and a friend, Colin Downs, were a trio. Colin lived on Frere Road, which was the next road to us on Fort Street. Colin lived with his mum and brothers. Trevor, Neville and sister Linda were on the third floor flat as well, which was only a small room which they rented for the five of them. They had lost their father earlier. Neville was the eldest, and then there was Trevor, Colin and Linda. Their mum was quite a simple Anglo Indian woman with very little education and very poor. She wasn't bothered if her kids went to school and pampered them to stay at home as she was quite lonely without a husband.

Colin, Neville and Trevor went to St Peter's School, Byculla, for a while, and Trevor was the most intelligent of the lot and used to read endless novels till all hours of the night under the street lamppost. Linda, who was a very simple girl and very innocent, was like a sister to Jim and me. She had no education at all but did all the housework and cooked for her brothers and mum in the tiny flat of theirs. She and her brother Colin were great jivers, and I remember Linda getting out of breath when she was about 15 or 16 years old and being very skinny and poor. She did not have very nice clothes or shoes as a young girl should, so my sister Maureen used to hand down Linda some of her clothes and shoes. Linda and Colin used to practice their jiving in their tiny apartment and became very good at it and won a few jive contests. At the same time, my sister Jean and her partner, Dougie Quighly, were red-hot jivers, also winning a lot of jive contests.

Linda in the 1960s came to England and was married but died very soon after from a hole in her heart. We were all very sad as we loved her very much.

The Pound Parties

Dougie Quighly taught me my first lessons in the jive. I learnt to do the flaps, where you flap your knees to and fro like flapping your wings. I got really good at it, so I used to go for pound parties, where everyone pitched in a pound or whatever eats you wanted to contribute to the pound party. So Colin Downs and a few other Anglos pooled in for about two or three pounds of *buggias* (a sort of onion *baaji* dish), which we bought from the buggia wallah, who cooked them in a large wok about three feet in diameter and wrapped them up in newspaper, which we took to the pound party. The party was held in Kenny Gustad's house with his stepsister Solveigh and lots of Anglo girls, so we started the party with Kenny's electric radio gram, a rare item heard of in those days as it was only affordable by those who were well off, which Kenny's parents were but were never there, so we had the place all to ourselves. The party went on till early hours of the morning with records of Elvis, Little Richard, Fats Domino, Bill Haley and others, and we all jived till we dropped and, of course, not forgetting the booze and the hangovers the next day.

L/R Me, Colin Downs & bro Jimmy & Bunny

Our Gang

My brother Jim, Colin Downs and I formed a regular get-together and called ourselves the Starzy Gangzy because we started smoking Star brand of ciggies. We used to meet up and roam all over and visit the jukebox joints at Colaba Causeway and smoked our Star fags. We used to bunk school and steal comic books and sell them to the rich Indian boys at school.

We made enough cash to enable us to go to the movies, including the Sunday morning movies at the Regal Cinema or the Strand or the New Empire or the Metro and even the Rex Cinema, where they showed Indian movies in Hindi dialogue with famous actors and actresses like Raj Kapoor, Dilip Kumar, Nargis, Madhubala, Dev Anand and Nimmi, who were some of the great all-time legends of the Indian movies. We used to get in free to the Rex Cinema as they knew my dad and mum because we lived opposite to the Rex Cinema. The manager allowed us in free of charge. We used to sit in the Rex movie house in the front seats, which consisted of benches in rows. Since we were allowed in free, we could not complain and just made ourselves as comfortable as possible with all those smelly and poor Indians who smoked beedies (a poor man's cigar) and ate paan during the movie, but we enjoyed the movies. We started to learn some of the Indian songs from the movies as nearly all the Indian movies had songs in them.

Then there were the Indian *chokra* boys. They were very poor lads who were orphaned and lived on the odd jobs they got on the docks as chipper painters. They lived on the streets and slept on the pavements as slum dogs. Their home was the streets, and lots of them lived below our building. We got to know some of the regular ones by their nicknames as they used to playfully tease us when we were schooling and speak to us in their Pigeon English, which they picked up from us or others, such as shuddup, bloody fool, basket for bastard and puck arf instead of fuck off. But we had a lot of fun with them, and some of those who were older than us and more matured wanted to be our friends and protect us from any bullies or anytime we had bother with anyone. These guys would offer to protect us as minders, only because they lived below us and knew our parents and sisters and out of respect would never let any harm come to us. Some of them, even though being a Hindu or Muslim, would want to come with us to the midnight Mass service and dress up in their glad rags during the Christmas break.

Our house had paper decorations during Christmas, and so had the streets and restaurants that were all illuminated. Even though the Hindus and Muslims all celebrated together, we were all brothers. The streets were decorated with large paper 'stars' about three feet by three feet made of fine tissue paper, and inside them were either candles or electric bulbs of different colours. After the midnight Mass, we used to go 'carol', singing in a 'Garywallah', a coach (which was a horse-driven coach with leather seats and a canopy covering at the rear). We used to sit with the driver of the gariwallah on the top front seats and be 'high' on the local 'country' liquor, which was the illegal stuff we bought from the 'aunties' who sold the liquor in the corner shops. We called them aunties out of respect. Why? I will never know, but that is what they were called, and the country liquor was sometimes called snake juice as it was 100 per cent proof and tasted like shit. To take away the bad taste and smell, the aunties gave us a bit of fried fish or curried fried meat. We used to buy this country booze in small bottles like a hip flask and take them with us to the open-air dances held at the Bombay Gymkhana, which started around 9 p.m. or 10 p.m. and finished at 6 a.m. Sometimes one or two of the well-dressed 'chokra boys' came to these dances as well, mainly to look after us and feel proud and important.

Besides my brother Jim, Colin and I used to meet up with a few Anglo boys. Peter was one of them, a white-skinned Anglo with blue eyes and blond hair, and we called him Peter the Bent Neck as he had a habit of leaning his head to one side because he thought he looked cool. Now Peter, being the fairest, was a bit of a pretty boy, and there was a guy who was gay and preyed on young boys. He was very wealthy. He had a convertible Mercedes and fancied the company of young Anglo boys. He drove up one evening and saw us boys hanging around the jukebox joint and stopped to ask us for some directions. Then he asked us if we didn't mind showing him the way, so all four of us hopped in this swish car and started to enjoy the ride. After we got him to his destination, he said thanks and said he'd like to meet up again sometime. We said sure, and the next thing we knew, he was picking us up quite frequently for drives to posh places like Malabar Hills for ice creams (a rare item for us boys). The best part was he fancied Peter because he was the fairest with blue eyes and blond hair and wanted Peter in the front seat with him whilst the rest of us sat at the back. We enjoyed the drive in this posh convertible and taken to all the posh restaurants, where we smoked and drank all the best stuff. Peter would not go alone with this gay guy, whose name we did not know. We didn't care if he was gay as long as we were treated well and no harm came to Peter or any of us.

MY INDIAN GIRLFRIEND

I met a chick named Zena at an Indian function. She was a pretty young girl with fair skin and black hair. Colin, Jim, Peter and I found out that there was a 'wedding' going on at the Cowsee Jehanghir Halls, and these weddings usually consisted of weddings. When we boys found out about this wedding, we decided to invite ourselves to it, so we dashed off home and started to tog up for this wedding. We rushed back to it, and to make it look authentic, we wrapped up a so-called gift so as we entered, it would look good. The gift for the bride and groom would be anything wrapped up in a box and covered with wrapping paper or any other rubbish we could think of. They would say thank us and told us to go and enjoy the rest of the wedding with free drinks and food and music for dancing. The Indian girls knew we were famous for our jiving, and when the music started, we would pick up a delicious Indian chick, and then we were like 'John Travolta' on the dance floor, and the Indian dames (we used to call chicks dames) would be lining up to dance with us.

Then that was where I met Zena, this innocent fair dame who was really coming on to me, especially in the slow dances. What with me and my hard-on, we were well away, so much so that she wanted to see me again. I had no such luxuries as a phone, so I told her where I lived and to meet me near the billiard salon, where I usually hung out. Zena turned up the very next day, and boy was I gobsmacked. Being an Indian dame, she was well off and arrived by taxi (the yellow and black ones). I could just about afford bus or tram fares, and she rolled up in a taxi. Well, what more could I say but hurry along to her before the rest of the boys hanging around would start giving me some stick? So I dashed off, red-faced and embarrassed, before any of the boys could say anything. These 'dates' with Zena went on for a few weeks until I discovered whilst passionately kissing and tongue kissing Zena that I was getting a peculiar odour of something not very nice, and this odour was putting me off her a little, and I started to back off, and she asked what the matter was. I'd make some excuse and said I was not feeling too well, and I headed off home. I never ever saw Zena again.

Then a couple of years later, Jane matured, and she used to wear expensive perfumes such as 'Worth' and also arrive by taxi to pick me up, and of course, my brother Jim would tag along for the ride to the movies or wherever we fancied going. She would treat us as she was always loaded with cash supplied by her rich auntie, a white Anglo Indian who supplied rich Indians with imported 'Johnny Walker' or any other services they required. Jane came to inherit some of the cash benefits from her rich aunt. As for me, she also gave me some spending money. 'No questions asked' as I understood this was a common procedure and thought nothing more of it. My brother Jim and I were getting free outings, and sometimes Jane would buy Jim and me materials to have clothes made to measure by our tailor Joe Martin.

CHAPTER 8

THE PANI PURI WALLAH

Typical Pani Poori stalls

We also ate *pani puri* (small puffed purries filled with boiled small chick peas, chilli powder and tamarind sauce dipped in a sort of pepper water liquid). Very tasty indeed for the price of four annas for four. Boy, what a treat!

Some of the other treats were the *pancham poori wallah*, who did us four saucer-sized puris for four annas (£1 = 80 rupees, and there were sixteen annas in a rupee), so it was dirt cheap. With the

four puris, you got a bowlful of *dhal* (lentils). Some vegetables were
served by a dirty old waiter. We could have more dhal if we desired.
You could have as much dhal and vegetables as required with your
four puris, so we filled each mouthful of puris with as much dhal
as possible so as to have extra dhal and vegetables, at no extra cost.
Sometimes when we were broke, we used to share four puris between
the two of us. When we got home, we didn't bother with what was for
dinner as there wasn't much anyway as in those days. My mum was
just about keeping up with the rent to the landlord.

Sometimes Jim and I would eat with our Madrasi friend Velu, who
lived on the first floor of our building called Hotel Friends and rented
an apartment with loads of other Madrasi friends of his. Velu was a
very learned man and was studying law and is now a barrister. We
used to share his tiffin (an Indian lunch) delivered to him at lunch
and suppertime. He then used to give us some of his very interesting-
looking food to taste. That was when we got the feel for this Madrasi
food, which was very hot and spicy, but we loved it. Velu used to tease
us as we were Anglos compared with his dark-skinned Madras friends,
and he tried to sing English songs in his Madras accent, which was
really funny. He used to sing 'Delilah', and he went, 'Deelilah so
enchanting so fear', instead of 'fair', and we used to have a good laugh.
He couldn't say 'love'; instead, he'd say 'lowe' no matter how many
times we tried to correct him, but that was good old Velu. He still
keeps in touch with us from India till today. He's now married and has
a daughter.

The second floor of our building was more or less a warehouse
stocked with carpets by the cycle man on the ground floor, who also
did the Saata betting. There was another family from Madras with a
son called Sunny and a daughter called Kunjanama. Sunny boy used
to spend a lot of time at our place, so much so my mum named him
the seventh child.

Our landlord who lived to the right side of our flat was a Muslim.
He had a servant called Khambar. On Muslim feast days, he would
treat us to delicious vermicelli like I've never ever tasted before. In
other ways, he was very stingy. He turned off our electricity at 10

p.m. as that was the allowance with our rent. Once, when my uncle Peter Rocque came to visit and the lights went out at 10 p.m. by our landlord whilst he was having booze up with my dad, he'd go mad and, in a firm manner, ask the landlord to switch the lights back on, who would then switch them back on again. The landlord knew not to mess around with my uncle and didn't bother us after that.

THE BUJJIA WALLAH

The Bujjia wallah owned the corner little shop that sold *bujjias* (deep-fried potatoes or onions or chillies or brinjals in batter), a very tasty and cheap snack served to you in a sheet of newspaper with a chutney sauce. It would cost about two annas or four annas for a handful of bhujjias if we could afford it. A pound in weight would cost ten annas, which was our contribution to the 'pound parties'.

THE GOLA AND NARAYAL WALLAHS

The *gola wallah* was a vendor who sold crushed ice on a tabletop supported by four cycle wheels. He stuck the crushed ice which formed a ball onto a piece of stick and coated it with different-coloured syrups which cost about two or three annas. We would suck all the syrup off and would ask him to top it up with some more, which he did quite disgruntled, but we didn't care.

The *narayal wallah* was a man selling coconuts that were sold on the roadside from a basket he held up on his head. He'd take out a fresh coconut and shave off the top, scoop out the fresh coconut pulp inside the coconut and then give you the opened coconut to drink the refreshing and cool coconut water. You were in heaven!

THE GHUNNA WALLAH

There also was the *ghunna wallah*, who sold freshly squeezed sugarcane juice from a mobile cart built on four wheels from an old bicycle. Built onto the cart was a wooden framework, 6' x 5', and upon this framework was a huge metal grinder with cogged wheels. The two metal wheels spun around, squashing the raw sugarcane, which filled your glass with the coolest sugarcane juice with ice added. The liquid was the best that you ever tasted in your whole life, especially in the heat and the dust of good ol' Bombay.

CHAPTER 9

ST FRANCIS DE SALES AND BOARDING SCHOOL, NAGPUR, INDIA

M um got in touch with my uncle Mr Hackett, who was a very well-respected maths teacher in St Francis de Sales High School in Nagpur, India. My mum arranged for my brother Jim and me to enlist in the boarding school, and in the interim period of becoming boarders, Jim and I had to stay with my mum's sister Aunt Lizzie and her sons Rex and Jimmy. Now Rex was a very strict, a no-nonsense man and suffered with asthma. Jim and I, who were used to the lazy life of Bombay, did not want to wake up early as Rex did. He used to scream at us to wake up, saying repeatedly, 'Jimmy, Trevor, wake up!' several times and then explode. Eventually, at the very top of his voice, he would say, 'Jimmy, Trevor, get uuuupp!' Well, the whole neighbourhood must have heard him. Boy did we move it.

Aunty Lizzie didn't give us much hassle. She was more interested in what was going on next door as there was a 'tarty' dame living there who used to carry on with different blokes. Lizzie used to eavesdrop on her. This tart knew what Lizzie was up to and purposely went on teasing Lizzie and acted more and more like a tart. Once when Aunty Lizzie had her ear to the dividing partition made of a sort of canvas, we asked Aunty Lizzie what the matter was, and she said, 'Oh, I was just looking for my needle I had stuck into the canvas.' Jim and I must have stayed there for about two weeks until we finally moved into the boarding school.

My uncle Mr Hackett, the maths teacher, was the husband of my mum's sister Josephine, a big strapping woman compared with my small mum, and boy could she cook. She was strict but kind and generous with her food as she used to treat us on weekends with *burrah khana*, a feast of a meal with gorgeous helpings of parathas (a chapatti) fried with plenty of ghee (clarified butter) or beautiful *pillau* rice and gorgeous chicken or mutton curry and dhal or ball curry and yellow rice with *papadoms* and homemade pickles. We went back to boarding school real content.

In boarding school, we were served just dhal and rice every day till it came out of our ears, so to speak. We began to love it as boarders; it was different from the Bombay *goondas* (dropouts) that we were as for the first time, we were taught discipline and started living a regular life. We got up every day at 5 a.m., washed, dressed and were ready for daily Mass at the church, in our smart navy blue jackets and white trousers. At Mass, we kept eyeing up the convent 'chicks' who attended as well, in particular, a dame called Carmen Menass, whom I used to fancy. She used to give me the eye, but that was as far as it went because I was locked up, and so was she. I used to dream about her and was told by my cousin Barbara Jacobs from my mum's side that Carmen also fancied me, but there was no chance of us getting it on together. We were quite content with that.

I started to love boarding school. Apart from the dhal and rice every day, except for the weekends or on Saints days, we got *burra khana*, that is, proper meat or fish curry added with parathas and some *bhendi* (okras) or brinjals. The cook was an Anglo Indian boy named Charles, who had polio in his leg but a body like Charles Atlas. He was very strong at gymnastics, parallel bars and the roman rings. He was our PT instructor, but his cooking was excellent, and he used to cook up different varieties of dhal every day so much so I got to love it till today.

He also used to bake fresh bread rolls for breakfast we called them *gutlies*. We used to trade our fresh gutlies with the day scholar boys who traded them for homemade fresh parathas with lovely mutton curry inside, something like a kebab roll. The day scholars wanted to hear all about Bombay and the jukeboxes and how to jive, of course, talk about singing and girls, girls, girls. When my uncle Mr Hackett heard about the jukeboxes, he used to say 'Forget about those jukeboxes', as this was Nagpur, not Bombay, but he was a very kind and gentle man and paid special attention to us as my mum had told him all the trouble we gave her in Bombay, especially as my dad wasn't around to supervise us. We went from bad to worse, so Mr Hackett, who looked a bit like Edward. G. Robinson, swore to my mum he'd take care of us and straighten us out and our *ghand musti* (bad ways).

As I said, we were woken up at 5 a.m. every day. After daily Mass was breakfast and then study and prepare for evening classes. We broke up for lunch for some dhal and rice, some more ghutlies or homemade cakes for tea. Then we broke up classes around 4 p.m. and changed our uniform of white shirts and khaki pants (trousers) into our games outfits to play either football or hockey or cricket. I usually chose football as I had a massive hob with the ball, so I played defence. Bro Laurie Fernandes, who was a trainee priest, was a pretty tough character, and he used to train us in boxing, and when my turn came for boxing training and I refused, Brother Laurie said, 'Oh, I see you don't want to spoil your pretty mug.' I said, 'Too right. What will the girls say when they see my ugly mug?' He would give up on me and boxing as he knew I was a bit of a Caruso.

After games, we boys had to shower every day in cold water. We had to strip naked and step into line, about ten boys in a row, alongside each other about four feet apart under our own showerhead and another row of ten boys opposite us also four feet apart. The brother who was in charge allowed us about one or two minutes to run the water. He'd bang on the pipes again to stop the water. We had to start soaping ourselves. With the bunch of keys in his hand, he would bang on the metal pipes again as a signal for us to turn on the taps for another minute or two and then another bang on the pipes to turn the taps off. Showers lasted about five or six minutes.

In the meantime, whilst showering, some boys would start fooling around with one another and play games such as hiding the soap, or one boy would fancy another pretty boy and go to fondle him. Then one of them would end up with soap still on his body because of the mucking about, missing the bang to start the water after the soaping. He would end up having to wipe off the remaining soap with his towel. In any case, it was all a bit of school boys' fun and quite funny in a way.

After the showers, we had our supper of dhal and rice again, and some boys, including me, had our bottles of pickles from home, which we hid in our lockers in the dormitory where we slept, about ten beds, five feet apart. We got out our pickles, usually hot mango or chilli or hot lime pickle, and add it to our meals. Not all boys had pickles, so there were break-in to our lockers as they had none. We boys used to gather together and plan some mischief such as climbing over the walls at night to buy hot gram or peanuts, which we called monkey nuts, and when we were caught doing so, we were caned on our palms, about ten strokes by the principal, Father DeSa.

Once, we guys bunked over the wall at night to watch the late night movie *Picnic*, starring Kim Novak and William Holden, and returned about midnight. I couldn't sleep thinking of Kim Novak. We had made our beds up as if we were in it, stuffing pillows and blankets in the shape of our bodies as if we were there sleeping. After lights out, we got busy with our late night adventure, and the four of us all bunked over the wall, saw the movie and sneaked back in and tiptoed back to our beds. The next morning, our joys were turned to sorrows as we were all four asked where we were last night. On this occasion, not only did we get a canning, but we got bald crops as well. That taught us a thing or two.

Mr Hackett was not pleased to hear about our escapade and said we deserved what we got and let that be a lesson to us shameless boys. He used to smoke a pipe at intervals during our maths class, just like Edward. G. Robinson, and made us laugh. When the time came for our exams, he would point out the very important questions that would appear in the exam papers. He would look at me and give me a wink so as to say that particular question was a dead cert to come up in the exams. It sure did. I was useless at maths, not too bad in geometry and totally useless with algebra. When the exams day finally came, I was a bag of nerves and did the bits of the arithmetic and geometry and left out all the algebra papers, with the result I managed a pass and scraped through. I did well in English, art,

science and religious education, and on the whole, I managed to pass
my matriculation exams with no special grades. Mr Hackett insisted
I stayed on and went to college for further studies, but I said I had
had enough. He said, 'I know what you Bombay boys want. It's that
damn jukebox'. I still loved the man as he was very kind to us and
quietly gave us pocket money and said not to mention it to his wife.
Mr Hackett later on I discovered that he had donated a large grotto of
Our Blessed Virgin Mary to the church, which was on the forecourt of
the church entrance to St Francis De Sales Church and High School.

A total of forty years later, I visited my old boarding school, and
who did I see, Brother Laurie, but I couldn't remember his name. He
said to me, 'Oh, you pretty boy, you only remember the songs'. He was
now a reverend Fr Laurie Fernandes, the principal of SFS High School.
I shed a few tears and kissed and hugged him.

Besides him was another geography master, Sir Amarant, I also
visited and shed a few more tears. Old man Hackett had passed away,
and his family moved to Canada. I also visited the house where I was
born in Nagpur, which was my mum's house, and in it now lived
Dominic Francis, his wife (my cousin Barbara), her three sons and
Coral Anne. They treated us like royalty with special brain curry and
real big *burra khana*.

Myself 3rd from right, next to Errol Woods.

Start of my singing career

I was about 13 years old in Bombay at St Xavier's school in the choir, before Nagpur boarding school. My voice had broken; hence, I was not a solo singer with the choir anymore. They asked me to join the alto section, and that was where I learnt how to sing in harmony to any tune.

I entered for a singing contest at St Xavier's High School Fete with my friend Ronnie Menezes on piano. I sang '16 Tons' by Tennessee Ernie Ford, which was a hit in 1954. I won the first prize, and I was very pleased with myself, so was Ronnie. We used to practice other songs at his house as he had a piano. I also used to sing a lot of Johnnie Ray songs like 'Cry' and 'Faith Can Move Mountains'. Rock 'n' roll was nowhere on the scene.

During my boarding school days at Nagpur, one fine day during our break period in the evening, when we used to sit and relax and listen to the school radio played over the school speakers, I happened to hear this wonderful exciting singer who they called ELVIS PRESLEY. Who in the world had a name like that? I was totally gobsmacked, and his singing was something I never heard before as it was so different from any other singer I had ever heard. The song was 'My Baby Left Me'. Wow! Did it make every bone in my body shake with the rhythm. I didn't know what had hit me, and from then on, I wanted to know more about this so-called Elvis Presley. I returned back to Bombay in 1957, after finishing with boarding school in Nagpur.

On my arrival to Bombay at the movies, they were showing 'Love Me Tender' by this man Elvis Presley. I was ecstatic and was dying to see it. My brother Eddie had already seen it and said to me, 'Wow, Trev, you should see this guy Elvis. He can really move when he sings.' Eddie gave me a little demo on how Elvis moved, sort of swung his hips from side to side and flicked his legs as if they didn't belong to him. I said, 'Wow that is really something groovy and something we'd never seen by other singers like Perry Como, Frank Sinatra or Dean Martin.' Elvis was just Elvis. At first, I thought he was a bit like

Johnny Ray, who was my guru until Elvis came along.Bill Haley and His Comets were the first to bring out the crazy craze of rock 'n' roll with 'Rock around the Clock'. The cinema seats were ripped up with the mad excitement of rock 'n' roll as there was nothing to compare it with before. We all went crazy, until Elvis came along, then all hell broke loose with singers like Little Richard, Jerry Lee Lewis, Fats Domino, Chuck Berry and loads of others. Actually, it was Elvis who opened the doors to black singers like Little Richard, Chuck Berry and Fats Domino, so this was the craze that hit Bombay like a storm. The jive was taken over by the crazy dance of 'Rock 'n' Roll'. We copied the mad movements from *Rock around the Clock* movie at our Anglo dances and parties. We used to play the records at the jukebox joints and started to rock 'n' roll outside on the pavements. We just didn't give a damn as long as we were enjoying it.

The old tram days in Bombay, during the British Raj.

'THE TEENAGE ROCKERS'

To begin my story of the 'Teenage Rockers', well, when I got back from boarding school in 1957 and Elvis was a real hot property, I got this thing inside me that I wanted to be like Elvis, so I looked up my old pianist Ronnie Menezes and started to sing Elvis's 'Don't Be Cruel'. Ronnie thought I was doing a good job as Elvis and suggested we took our song to the Ovaltine Amateur Hour, a local radio station in Bombay which was relayed all over India. So we approached Hamid Sayani, who called himself the Ovaltine man. He was very impressed and agreed right away, and overnight we became famous and were the talk of the town in Bombay.

We then got this sudden idea that we should form our own rock 'n' roll group, with Ronnie's brother Russell who played the piano accordion and Colin Downs on drums and my bro Eddie on the 'box bass' (which was made out of an old Tea Chest about two and a half feet square, hollow inside with a cat gut tied to the centre of the box and the other end tied to a wooden pole). We got an amazing bass sound from it as we got together, had regular practices and were really getting good. We discussed what to call ourselves, and as we were all teenagers, we decided on 'Teenage Rockers'.

Now at the time, my sister Joyce worked at Glaxo Laboratories at Worli, Bombay, and she managed to get our group 'Teenage Rockers' our very first gig. Boy were we excited and raring to go, we managed to get transported from Ronnie's dad with our box base and a homemade drum kit and a new addition to our group Cedric Thorose on lead guitar, who had just come down to Bombay from Nagpur.

Cedric and I met at the boarding school in Nagpur, where he was a day scholar. He used to talk a lot about coming to Bombay, and he used to play guitar and sang like Pat Boone. Cedric also joined our group on his homemade electric guitar he made himself, was pretty good at it. Ronnie was the group leader. Being the only one who could read music and play the piano, he taught us boys how to sing in harmony. We sang 'Love Letters in the Sand' and 'Don't Be Cruel' with all the harmonies and with the wop bops, like Elvis and the Jordanairs. We were starting to get real popular after our first gig at Glaxo Labs. Then we went on to play for the *Times of India Show* after which we got a big gig at a place called Busaval on the outskirts of Bombay. It went down a bomb.

We continued to become popular and got another booking at the Bandra fare. The Teenage Rockers were in full swing. Then came along the Elvis Presley of Bombay contest held at the Taj Hotel, which

was a real posh joint, and one of the contestants was Roly Daniels
(a country and Western singer who has made a name for himself in
Ireland). There was Roly, me and a guy called Neville Peters and some
others who took part in the contest. Neville won the Senior Elvis, and
I won the junior title as I was under 18, and Roly got nowhere.Oh,
Bombay was rockin' in those days, what with the famous Teenage
Rockers, Roly Daniels with Abe and the Gaylads (they weren't really
gay, just happy lads), and numerous other groups kept coming up.
Someone arranged a rock 'n' roll jamboree at the Eros Cinema with
huge posters of us all in the foyer. We felt like movie stars. The show
was a smash hit, and although we did not get paid a lot, we were happy
just to do it. I used to grease my hair in the Elvis quiff, and before
that, it was the Tony Curtis style. Although we were really famous in
Bombay, we were not getting anywhere and weren't financially well
off either. We were just drifting along until my mum saw that I was
a talented young singer who was wasting my time in Bombay, so she
contacted my uncle in Delhi. His name was Frank Jacobs.

Ronnie Menezes the brainchild of "Teenage Rockers"
now a big name in Bombay, plays Jazz

A Very Young Teenage Rocker

CHAPTER 10

WENGER'S RESTAURANT
CONNAUGHT, CIRCUS, DELHI

FIRST MEETING WITH ZOE, THE GIRL OF MY DREAMS!

Uncle Frank lived at the President's Estate in New Delhi with his wife, Auntie Louise, and his kids. I was lodging with Uncle Frank and his family. Uncle Frank promised my mum to look after me and fixed me up to sing with a band at Wenger's Restaurant with Carl Mannet and his band. Carl played piano, Cedric Abernetti on double bass, Ronnie on trumpet, Johnny on sax, a drummer Tony Tarley and me doing the vocals of Elvis, Dean Martin, Paul Anka and others. Wenger's was swinging in the year 1958 with rock 'n' roll and jam sessions on Sundays. It was loaded with lots of pretty young college students, who started to fancy me. I didn't realise it until I started to receive fan mail from unknown females who wanted to date me. in the meantime, I met a Bengali girl who used to dress in saris, and her father was a big shot in Delhi. She was a real sexy looker and wanted more than just kissing and cuddling. She was the first girl I had to cope with and having to deal with undoing her sari. By the time I finally undid it, I lost interest. She was real hot stuff with other boys. I knew that she used to see other guys as well, but I was cool about it.

Since I was getting more and more popular with the women, my band leader, Carl Mannet, used me to pull the women and girls for the boys in the band, so each time a pretty girl would appear, Carl would say, 'Go on, Trev, give 'em the eye', so I would. Then later on, I would go and chat her up, but only to introduce her to the band boys.

Wengers Restaurant, Cannaught Circus, Delhi

A Very Young Zoe aged 14 and me, Love in Full Bloom!

One of the many girl fans I had happened to meet was a Punjabi girl, who came with her sister to hear me at Wenger's. She was crazy over me and made it quite clear. Her sister told me she was so crazily in love with me and wanted to marry me. She used to place fresh garlands of flowers around the picture I gave her of me, which she blew up to a giant size, but this romance didn't last as I wasn't into Punjabi girls, although she told me that if I married her and settled in Nairobi in her father's hotel business, I could be very wealthy. However, I didn't fancy that, so I turned her down. After I parted from her, she promised to write, and boy did she keep in touch with loads of love letters and reminding me of the marriage proposal and an offer to work for her father in his hotel business.

The love of my life turned up one sunny Sunday at the jam sessions with a real hot chick, Shirley was the hottest chick in town. All the guys were like lap dogs after her, but I was cool about her as I knew she was only after the rich guys. One day she happened to walk in with this other cool chick whom I'd never seen before, who was really well built but pretty as well as innocent-looking. She kept staring at me as if I was some kind of super star, and I sort of got the gist and played it real cool and said, 'Hi, babe, who's this gorgeous one with you? Never seen her before.' She said, 'She's my pretty little cousin who's come for a short visit from her hometown in Cawnpore.' I said, 'What's your name then, cousin?' And this shy little voice said, 'Zoe Phillipowsky.' I said, 'What? Never mind, I'll just call you honey. How does that grab you?' and she just went a bit red and nodded in approval, still not taking her eyes off me. I made the next move and to asked her if she didn't mind coming with her 'cousin Zoe' to a joint called Alps, where I used to hang out for a drink and chill out after my session at Wenger's. She agreed to bring Zoe to Alps and would meet me there. When I did finally got to Alps later on, the band was playing cool jazz. The joint was smoky and romantic. As I walked in, who did I see?

My old flame, the Bengali chic. As soon as she saw me, she flung her arms around me and started to dance with me real slow and sexily and giving it all. She behaved as if she hadn't seen me for ages. Then to my surprise, who should I see staring at me with dreamy eyes? This sweet-looking, innocent chick with her cousin. It was Zoe, the girl of my dreams. She was dancing with some other guy, I was dancing with the Bengali dame and Zoe was giving me the eye, although she was with this other guy. Then after the dance finished with her, I went over to Zoe and said, 'Hi, honey, it's me.' She very nervously said, 'Hi, it's good to meet you again. Do you fancy taking the floor with me?' When she got up to dance with me, I could see her sweet, innocent face, although she tried to look older than she actually was with some makeup. I could see she was real pretty, and boy, did she have some body on her!

I straight away felt her firm breasts against my chest and started to get very horny as I grabbed her tightly towards me. I was now getting very horny and excited. I could feel her hot breath, her sweet rosy lips parting open like a lotus flower, and then I caressed her face and placed my lips on hers. She started to blush, and then I pulled her closer and kissed her lips again and again. This time thrusting my tongue into her mouth and meeting her sweetest-tasting tongue for the first time. Man was I in heaven. This went on for quite a while until I could stand it no more and decided to leave Alps and take her somewhere more interesting. I paid the bill as the other guys she originally came with all left the joint and left without paying. I was the one left to settle up. They played me for a sucker as they got jealous of Zoe fancying me and not them.

I managed somehow to take Zoe to the movies and don't rightly remember what the movie was about, but we two lovebirds couldn't wait to get it together. Our lips must have become sore with all that smooching until I decided to take her someplace else for some real action, and where else could we go to as I was not too familiar with Delhi, so we took a rickshaw to the nearest gardens, which was quiet a place for lovers to bill and coo. I didn't waste much time and straight away started working on Zoe, hands running all over her body and getting all steamed up, until I got a bit rough and didn't realise I had broken her necklace, which broke into little beads all over the place. Then we discovered we were being watched by the watchman of the park, who told us to move on and to behave ourselves in a public place.

During this escapade, I happened to ask Zoe her age, and when she said she was 14, I just froze as all the time, I imagined her to be about 23. For an Anglo Indian girl, she sure was well developed in all the right places. I said, 'Do you want me to be locked up? You sure are under aged.' She just blushed shyly and ignored what I'd said.

Our romance went on for a few more days until I went to her cousin's house, and there, Zoe and I had another amorous session, this time on the terrace above on the roof of the building, kissing, French style and more but no sex yet as we both didn't want to cross that line.

Our romancing was cut short as Zoe's mum in her hometown, Cawnpore, decided to bring Zoe home as she had heard about her daughter's amorous goings-on with this 'singer' in Delhi. She was only 14 and well below the age of consent and was still a schoolgirl, going out with this 18-year-old singer from BOMBAY of all places. WOW, that was it for me, a short but sweetest romance I ever experienced for the very first time and didn't realise I was in love for the very first time as well.

Ever since I met Zoe, nothing ever mattered to me with other girls. Jane was just my woman, and the Bengali dame was just a common tart of Delhi with all the boys running around her like lap dogs. Yes, I think I was finally changing my opinion of women after meeting Zoe. She seemed the most pure and innocent type of girl I ever met, and my feelings for her were for the first time different as I was starting to fall in love for the very first time in my life with this simple and pure girl from the country.

Then suddenly, Zoe was out of my life for the time being as she was whisked away back to Cawnpore by her mum, but before she was taken back to Cawnpore, her wonderful cousin was trying to fix Zoe with a job at a posh hotel in Delhi as a trainee hairdresser to work with rich Indian male customers who wanted general hair, manicure and any other treatments on offer. Whilst Zoe was working on one of the rich Indian male clients who happened to be an old, balding man, she was shampooing his hair, and during the process, the rich client got carried away with this lovely young Anglo Indian girl working on his head. He started to run his hands up her legs as he thought nothing of it and that it was part of the treatment to get special extra thrills that would work with girls who were used to being touched up but not so with Zoe.

She immediately withdrew herself from this dirty old man and slapped his fat wet face with all her strength of a country girl. The guy was in total shock and demanded an apology from the owner of this establishment, saying he had never been so insulted in his entire life. Zoe, of course, was asked to leave immediately and was told by the boss that this sort of treatment was expected from rich clients and that she was not the type of girl they wanted in their establishment. So Zoe left them as soon as she could, and that was the end of her 'hairdressing career'.

Zoe and I kept in touch with a string of love letters to each other, but in the meantime, the female fans consisting of the local college students kept coming to see this Elvis-looking and cute teenage singer at Wenger's. I started to get anonymous fan mail from these college girls, but I was not aware of these letters as my uncle, who is expired now, when I was residing with, at the President's Estate, had been hiding my fan mail from me because it was his trump card as he did not want me to leave Delhi. I was offered a contract in Kashmir with the Carl Mannet Band. My uncle Frank was also having fun and used to come to Wenger's.

Auntie Louise was the chief matron at the Wellington Hospital in Delhi and commanded much respect from her staff and doctors. That was when she found out that I had trouble with my discharging left ear and trouble in hearing, so she had a word with one of the senior ear specialists. He had me in for an examination, after which a famous doctor Rao performed a major mastoid operation to my left ear, which lasted five hours. The doctor discovered during the operation that the infection in my ear was heading to my brain, which would cause serious problems. He managed to save my life but couldn't save my hearing in the left ear, which left me hard of hearing from then on. I somehow carried on with my singing at Wenger's, a few months after the operation, with my dodgy hearing, which I ignored at the time as I was just 18 years old and didn't worry about the loss of hearing that much. I carried on life as normal as possible.

I had stayed at Uncle Frank's house with my cousins for a whole year until I moved on to Kashmir for my next contract. Of course, my uncle Frank was not too happy with my leaving. That was when he came up with my unknown 'fan mail'.

He handed me a big pile of fan mail from different females who wrote to me expressing their desires to make love to me, with attached phone numbers and other details of their bust measurements and how they loved the way I sang so sexily and closed my eyes and sang so dreamily that they even dreamt about me, but there were so many of them I didn't know who to start with or where.

In the meantime, I got the news of the contract to Kashmir and made the journey to Jammu (a stop before Srinagar, Kashmir). We were in Jammu a couple of months at a joint called the Cosmos Hotel. I moved on to Srinagar, Kashmir.

A teenage Trevor Taylor in Kashmir, Srinagar, with The
Carl Mannet Band Cedric Thorose on guitar, Valley
on drums and Johnny on sax, Carl on piano.

Another picture of the Carl Mannet Combo with
Eric Kane on guitar, Val on trumpet, Tony Tarley on
drums, Carl on piano and me with guitar.

CHAPTER 11

JAMMU, NEXT STOP, SRINAGAR, KASHMIR

At the Cosmos in Jammu, we had a lot of fun. I met a guitarist named Eric Kane, who was new to the band; a female singer, Flora Brooks, from Calcutta; the usual sax player, Johnny; a trumpet player and a drummer named Tony Tarley. We had ballroom cabaret artistes, Sam and Ruby, and their kids Edwin and Salome, who were young teenagers who gave cha-cha and samba exhibitions. There were lots of entertainments every day, not forgetting the booze that I forgot to mention in Delhi. We used to drink 'Golden Eagle', a fabulous lager and coming from Bombay, where there was prohibition. I was in seventh heaven. All we had to do was snap our fingers at the waiter, and he'd bring us this Golden Eagle on a platter, cool as ice, for which I just signed a slip that was deducted from my monthly wages. I had nothing else to spend my money on as we were given full board and lodge by the hotel. I used to send most of my money home to my mum in Bombay, which she saved up for my fare towards my passage to England.

There was an army base at Jammu. The army officers of the Indian army used to come there with their wives to our hotel for an evening's entertainment. Of course, there was dancing and drinking and the usual cabaret floor shows by Sam and Ruby or Edwin and Salome.

One army officer's very attractive wife in a beautiful sari could not keep her eyes off me. What she saw in skinny old me I'd never know, but she kept staring at me with lust in her eyes I started to get worried, but by then, Tony the drummer and Carl Mannet started to egg me on as they noticed how this beautiful, lustful, busty woman was giving me the eye. I got even more nervous as her husband was observing his wife's behaviour, so he called the waiter and sent a drink for me with a note, inviting me to meet him and his wife for a chat.

My heart by now was in my mouth, and I was scared stiff. I didn't know what to expect, but I plucked up enough courage and went over to their table. 'My wife seems fascinated by you, my friend. What is your name?' 'Trr . . . ee . . . vv . . . oo . . . rr Ta . . . yy . . . loo . . . rr,' I said nervously. He said, 'Relax, my friend, and have a drink with us.' So I did and started to settle down until he said, 'Would you like to dance with my wife? She really wants to.' He said, 'Sure, go ahead, take the floor and make her day and mine.'

I very nervously took her hand and led her onto the dance floor, and the lights went dim. She was pressing her voluptuous body close to mine. Her husband kept on drinking and smiling at us as he looked pleased that his wife was getting her pleasures. She opened her rosy lips and started breathing real heavy and wanted to kiss me full-on, but I was turning away in embarrassment. Carl and the band boys were egging me on, but they didn't have to put up with her giant of a man, her husband, who could make minced meat out of me. I just about managed to kiss her wet lips and saw a few stars but drew away quickly before I could get carried away.

'Did you enjoy my wife's dancing? You must come to the officer's mess soon as my wife would love to see you and dance with you again.' I did go to the officer's mess, but again, this time I was in a mess as she wanted the full works from me. I was too scared and legged it the hell out of there, what with the army base and all that ammunition, I could be blown up to bits. I never saw either of them again.

Tony Tarley, the drummer, was an Anglo Indian strapping young lad who was of Phillipino decent and was a real fun guy, but Ruby, the dancer, fancied Tony and wanted to have an affair with Tony, so Tony obliged her with some amorous nights. Sam, her husband, was quite pleased as long as his wife was happy.

Then there was Flora Brooks, the new female singer whom Carl Mannet fancied, but she fancied the new guitarist, Eric Kane. Carl got really jealous, although he had his wife, Lynette, and daughter on the premises with us. Eric and I used to share a room, and Eric used to tell me all his secret love meetings with Flora and how Carl was so jealous and wanted to get rid of him.

Eric and I used to smoke *ganja* (dope), which in Kashmir was a very pure and good quality. Eric and I used to get real high on the stuff, but I didn't like it too much as it slowed me down, and I preferred the Golden Eagle instead. Carl didn't like us smoking the stuff, so he finally got rid of Eric. Before Eric could go back to Calcutta, he asked if he would like to accompany me to Cawnpore to visit Zoe as I was missing her. Eric and I took a couple of weeks off and went down to Cawnpore to meet Zoe and her folks.

The local guys in Cawnpore were like hound dogs around Zoe's house, sniffing after either Zoe or her sisters. One of the guys tried to scare me and tell me that Zoe's dad was a Shikari hunter who shot wild boars and tigers. If he didn't like me, he'd get out his twelve-bore shotguns, but that didn't scare me as I suspected they were jealous and went on ahead to meet her mum and dad. It turned out that Zoe's dad, Edwin, who later passed away in 1960 in England, turned out to be a really nice guy and welcomed me with a drink and showed me all the tigers and wild boars he shot, and we got on really well. God bless his soul.

Zoe's Dad Edwin Walter Phillipowsky
at Cawnpore, India

Zoe's Eldest sister Olga and husband Eddie Chapman's
60th wedding Anniversary in the UK

Olga and Eddie Chapman's youngest daughter Lisa,
sadly passed away, she liked my singing.

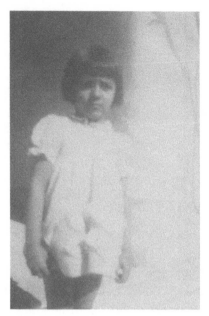

Zoe a little tearaway aged 2/3
in Agra, India.

The Beautiful Taj Mahal in Agra where Zoe was born in 1944.

Zoe, aged 14 and cousin
Shirley Beaulau in Delhi, India.

Whilst on my short stay in Cawnpore, Zoe and I had a lot of catching up to do. She fixed Eric and me with some lodgings for our short stay. During this time, Zoe and I had some very amorous times but never ever attempted to go all the way, very nearly but not all the way. Zoe's mum was different to me and made me quite welcome but didn't seem too keen on Eric, maybe because he was dark-skinned. That's how it was with some Anglo Indian families. Just because they were a bit fair-skinned, they were prejudiced against someone darker than them. It was the same with my mum. It seemed to stem down from the British ways. My mum used to tell me not to associate or play with the darker Indian boys or our servants, but I didn't see anything wrong with it and paid no attention to my mum. Even to speak the Indian language was considered a shame, but I didn't see it that way. I loved speaking Hindi and learnt Hindi songs from the Indian movies.

Zoe and I parted very sadly as my leave was up and returned to Jammu and prepare for my new contract in Srinagar, Kashmir.

The Premier Hotel, situated near the Dhal Lake in Kashmir, was the 'crem dela crem' of a place. We were a hit from the time we landed, what with all those beautiful Kashmiri chicks, which we dare not even try to chat up as we later on discovered that the big made Kashmiri guys didn't want us guys to interact with their women. As later on, we were confronted with an encounter in an alleyway and had a nasty experience when they threatened us with knives.

It all started with a beautiful Kashmiri chick named Nimmi, who started writing anonymous fan mail letters to little old me, and of course, I felt I wasn't losing my grip on the female chicks and quite proud of myself. I started to meet Nimmi and kissed and cuddled a couple of times until the encounter with the Kashmiri guys in the alley.

In Kashmir, there was an American army base, and we met this yank called Bruce, who was a strapping six footer, very fit and muscular compared with the rest of us band guys. Bruce was drinking with us, and after our late night show, we decided to take a stroll to the back streets of Srinagar to get Bruce some Kashmiri dope and have some fun, but that turned out not so funny as on our way back to the hotel, we were confronted in this dark alley by a gang of six to eight Kashmiri guys. They started threatening us with their knives and telling us in their funny accent to leave their women alone, or there would be bloodshed.

We started to back off and were getting ready to leg it, until Bruce, the tough yank whom we then discovered was this karate expert, told us not to worry and stay as we were. It was all right for him to say that as we were puny and not such fit guys. We were only musicians and didn't have a clue about fighting. In other words, we were shitting ourselves, scared stiff. Until in a flash, this crewcut superman of a man went into action, and we couldn't believe our eyes what we were experiencing. This hunk of a man started to lay into this Kashmiri lot with his superfast karate kicks and chops all we could do was watch in awe and gobsmacked at the way this yank floored them. He broke a few arms and legs whilst he was at it. The remaining Kashmiris started to leg it as they didn't want any more from Bruce, our Superman. We didn't have any more bother with them again as the Kashmiri police were now looking into how these guys were injured and by whom. Whilst in hospital, they were claiming they were beaten up by us and this big yank, but after a while, it all died off. We didn't have any more bother with the Kashmiris or the cops.

My courting with Nimmi slowed down as I didn't want any more encounters with the Kashmiri lot, so for a while, I lay low and started to think and write to Zoe, who was still in Cawnpore and preparing with her family to leave for England. All those love letters from Zoe to me and vice versa with letters full of lipstick kisses and some photos and promises of our undying love to each other forever.

Left to right, Cedric Thorose,
Roly Daniels and me, Indian Cowboys!

Valley (drummer), Cedric, Roly, me and
Johnny (Sax player) (left to right)

Whilst in Srinagar, Kashmir, I met up with other band guys
such as Roly Daniels, now a famous country singer in Ireland, doing
very well for himself. Roly and me and another Anglo called Cedric
Thorose used to go horse riding in Kashmir together, but Roly and I
were really rivals as he did the same Elvis stuff as I did. Then Cedric
later on joined my band with the Carl Mannet Combo. Roly's love
was really Country and Western music. Later on, when I finally met
Roly at a nightclub in England, he told me he was going to Ireland as
he wasn't having much luck in England, but I told Roly that I thought
Country and Western was too boring for me at the time and preferred
more exciting rock 'n' roll instead.

Cedric Thorose was now the new guitarist as Carl Mannet finally got rid of my old pal Eric Kane because of his carrying on with Flora Brooks, so that was the end of Eric and Flora.

My fun in Kashmir was now coming to the end of my contract, having met a lot of important people in my time there, including General Thamaya of the Indian army and Pundit Nehru, to name a few. I told the boss of Premier's, Mr Sony, that I was immigrating to the UK for good and didn't want to stay on. He had offered to double my salary and to forget about going to the UK as he didn't think I was doing the right thing and that by doing so, I would regret it. He advised me; he had been to England several times on business trips, knew all about the English prejudice and how they would call me a wog, insult me and tell me to go back to where I came from. If, however, I didn't like it in England, I would be welcomed back to Kashmir with double salary and live like a king. I was very tempted to take up his offer, but by then, I corresponded with my mum and discovered I had sent her enough money to pay for my brother Eddie and my passage to England.

I told the boss, Mr Sony, that I wanted to see my mum, whom I hadn't seen for a year and wanted some leave that was due to me and to think about extending my contract. He agreed to let me go and to think about signing another contract when I got back from Bombay. After visiting my mum and family, I never went back.

CHAPTER 12

OFF TO BLIGHTY

Whilst in Bombay again, I started to resort to my old *gunda* (layabout) ways and at the same time started to prepare for my passage to England together with my brother Eddie. My mum had made our Indian passports ready and had our passages to England booked on a very cheap cargo ship, *The Laos*. This was an Italian boat and full of Chinese passengers, who were filthy and kept eating hard-boiled eggs and dropping the eggshells all around the decks of the ship. We had to sleep on bunks in a common dormitory and were served sloppy meals on metal trays with compartments for each item of food and had to queue up like prisoners. I don't remember having a decent shower or shave in all the two or three weeks that we were on board the ship. We were given just £5 in the year 1960, which was all the foreign exchange we were allowed to take to England.

Whilst on board this ship with my brother Eddie and a friend of Eddie's called Alf, Mervin Donogue, me and a few Chinese guys got together, made our own entertainment and started to sing rock 'n' roll songs of Elvis, Bill Haley, Chuck Berry, etc. We had no guitars or anything of the sort. We just banged the beat on the deck floor and had a few cheap liquors we got from the ship's galley as £5 was worth quite a bit in 1960. When we docked at Port Said, it was full of prostitutes, which reminded me of old Bombay. I remembered leaving Bombay docks with my mum waving us goodbye endlessly. We passed the 'Gateway of India' with tears rolling down my eyes as we watched Bombay turn into a little dot.

We were on a 'boat train', which meant our boat took us as far as Marseilles in France, and then we had to catch a ferry boat to Dover in England and then a train to Paddington Station, where my sister Joyce and my beloved Zoe would be waiting for us. At Marseilles, Mervin Donogue was fascinated by those gorgeous French chicks and said he was staying put and wasn't interested in going any further to England. We told him not to get so carried away and to think about his future in England. Somehow we managed to change his mind; he carried on with us with much regret.

We finally arrived at Paddington Station looking like ex-cons, filthy dirty. I had grown a bit of a beard, so much so that neither Zoe nor Joyce could recognise me. Then when I saw Zoe, I could hardly recognise her or my sister Joyce. It had been more than a year since I had seen Zoe and about three years my sister Joyce. Zoe was looking so gorgeous that I thought she was some movie star with a totally different beehive hairdo, which was the fashion then, and looking like a beatnik. It was also the trend with heavy eye makeup and eyeliner. She still looked a million dollars and smelt of something just out of a rose garden, and she didn't care how I looked or smelt and gave me the most tender, loving hug and kisses that I had longed for so long.

No: 9 Cranleigh Gardens, South Kensington, London.

Our First Stay on ground floor flat

Joyce then got my bro Eddie, Zoe and me into a taxi to No 9, Cranley Gardens, South Kensington, to stay in a rented bedsit, at the cost of nine guineas a week. In 1960, it was considered very expensive. Joyce also bought Eddie and me lovely woollen overcoats each as we arrived with no woollies or proper clothes for the English weather. We were shivering like mice on that cold, damp, cloudy and grey day in England on that ninth of November 1960.

When we were arriving before Paddington Station, I noticed the houses in England for the first time with aerials on their rooftops and smoke out of chimneys, something I'd never seen in old Bombay. The houses all looked like something you see on *Coronation Street*. It sure gave me the creeps that I wanted to do a U-turn back to Bombay and started remembering Mr Sony's words: 'They will call you a wog and nigger and tell you to go back where you came from and not make you welcome at all'. I had left India, Bombay, Delhi and Kashmir, where I was living like a king, only to be insulted by these ignorant pigs. Oh, how I wanted to go back. What a great mistake I had made. I could have been a big Bollywood star, rich and famous, but I was here now with Zoe and Joyce coaxing me. I managed to be swayed, but in my heart, I could only think of India and wondered if I would ever return.

Cigarettes were very expensive, and of course, Zoe used to supply me with Senior Service fags as that was the brand available at the time. We were so short of money. Joyce used to tell Zoe off for bringing me fags instead of food. Eddie and I were sharing this bedsit and one single bed, a sink and a one-ringed cooker to warm up our soups or other tinned food. So Joyce was right, we shouldn't waste it on fags.

Zoe used to visit me from Croydon, which was an hour's journey to Kensington. I didn't have a clue how far or how safe it was. She was a 15- or 16-year chick and travelling all that distance on her own. I hadn't the slightest idea of the danger or the distance she was travelling to meet me, which I later on experienced when she told me how to get to West Croydon to visit her instead.

She told me to take a train to West Croydon. I was very nervous travelling for the first time on an English train alone, so as soon as I saw a station, 'West Norwood', I decided it was West Croydon in error in my nervous state. I got off the train. After asking several instructions of how to get back to West Croydon, I finally arrived about two hours later than planned. Zoe had nearly given up waiting but finally melted when she saw me.

I was now in West Croydon, and it was completely different from the posh area of South Kensington, and you know what? In November 1960, there was just one Indian restaurant on Derby Road, West Croydon, called the Curry House. It was the only place you could get a decent curry, and to make matters worse, there wasn't a single shop that sold Indian ingredients for you to cook your own curry. Compared with today, you cannot count the number of Indian stores and restaurants. They occupied every square inch of ground available, so much so you couldn't find a single English-owned shop or restaurant.

Apart from the Indian shops and restaurants, I bumped into an old pal I knew from Bombay. He was a cousin of my old flame Jane. He invited me to his place at Streatham SW 16 to try some of his home cooking of dhal, rice and Pilchard fish curry. Immediately, my mouth started watering, and I couldn't wait to accept his invite, which I did immediately, and boy did I get the treat of my life. After about two months without curry and the smell of it, I was in old Bombay again.

He shared a flat with his mum and sister at Baldry Gardens, SW 16, and asked me if I'd wish to stay with them and share the rent. I said I'd think about it as I was staying at the place of Zoe's mum at Campbell Road, West Croydon, and was looking for a job to get my feet on the ground.

Looking for a job, the Elvis Presley of Bombay, who never ever worked manually in any job until I left India?

I was remembering Mr Sony's words: 'You will never like England. You lived like a king in Kashmir, and now you will have to really work for your money. They will call you a wog or Paki and tell you to go back where you came from'.

Did I want to return to Kashmir on double my old salary and live like a king? Yes, I did and was getting the urge to bugger off back, away from this cold and damp Godforsaken country. I dreamt about curry; instead, it was just bloody fish and chips and cold insipid food; I felt it was not even fit for a dog.

Zoe & Me Early days 1960 in the UK

Three Bros Jim, Me & Eddie early 1960 UK.

My Very First Job in England

I stayed at the house of Zoe's mum for about two months and was forced to look for work. Zoe's mum used to make me sandwiches as a packed lunch for the day as I tried to spend the day looking for a job. Looking for a job was a joke in itself as I had no experience of work whatsoever and totally inexperienced, so I went along Purley Way, Croydon, knocking on every factory door, only to be told 'no vacancies', or was it my brown skin that put them off? I'd never know. I carried on my search for a job, the next few days without any luck, until I decided to get smartened up and wear a full suit, and maybe this would impress them to give me a job.

Until I came upon a factory called C. Baker Instruments. There was a board outside which read 'Cleaner required. Apply within'. I thought, *Why not? It's a start.* I didn't care anymore that I was the king of Bombay; I was desperate for work and money. I felt like 'the prodigal son', so I humbled myself and rang the bell. The door opened, and a tall rugged English man said, 'Can I help you?' 'Yes, yes,' I said nervously. 'I've come for the job advertised outside.' He said, 'That's for a cleaner. Did you want that?' 'Yes, yes, indeed, the cleaner's job if you'll have me.' He then said to me, 'You look too clean for a cleaner's job.' I said that he shouldn't be fooled by my smart appearance and that I would come for work in the appropriate work clothes to work as a cleaner. What must Mr Sony be thinking and laughing his head off, saying, 'I told you so.'

Tony was the foreman of C. Baker Instruments, who seemed somehow a nice guy to me with a kind yet stern, rugged appearance, and asked me, 'Are you Anglo Indian?' I was really shocked at this question. It was the very first time someone asked me that since I set foot in England. 'Yes, yes, I'm an Anglo Indian. How did you know?' 'Well, one more of you wouldn't make a difference. I already have a load of your kind inside. Could you start work Monday morning at eight as a bench fitter and not as a cleaner as advertised? There are a load of you so-called Anglos, and one of them could show you the ropes. All you have to do is get stuck in.' 'Thanks a ton, mister. I'll be here Monday mornin'.' 'You do that' was his reply.

I was in shock as I was returning to tell Zoe and her mum the good news. I finally got a job to start work on Monday. I was elated. I began to feel like somebody again, somebody up there liked me.

Tony the foreman was a really nice guy from the start. He filled me in as what to do on the production line of preparing microscope parts for painting and assembly. The wages were £7.50 per week, and with bonus for doing the job quicker, I could earn a bit more. So it went from Monday to Friday, with me and all these other Anglos. I knew some of them as I was earlier introduced to them by Zoe as she arrived in England six months or so prior to my arrival. I got to know this Anglo family known as the Young family. Winston and Keith were brothers, and Keith had fancied his chances with Zoe before I arrived in the UK.

My First job at C. Baker Instruments on scooter.

Zoe and I were sharing the flat at 15 Campbell Road. I was paying for board and lodge to Zoe's mum. Zoe had a job as a shop assistant in Croydon. Zoe and I had some money coming in from our jobs and started going for movies and dances at the Orchid Ballroom at Purley, the Locarno at Streatham SW 16 and the Hammersmith Palais every Thursday night.

In the meantime, Zoe and I got very intimate during my stay with Zoe's mum at Campbell Road, which now resulted with Zoe missing her periods. This got us worried, that she may be pregnant. This was when Zoe decided to arrange for me to stay with Dougie Fordham and his wife at Bensham Lane.

Dougie and his wife was an older Anglo Indian couple from Cawnpore India. They took my brother Eddie and me in as boarders. We stayed there for a few months until Zoe and I decided to get married.

I worked at Baker Instruments, which now changed its name to Vickers Instruments, on Purley Way. Whilst at Vickers on the assembly line, I made a friend of Winston Young, who got fond of me as we sang Elvis songs whilst we worked, so when Tony the foreman asked me one time in his cockney accent to fetch him a ''ammer', I asked Winston what Tony just said. Winston explained that Tony wanted a 'hammer' instead of a ''ammer'. Then later on, Tony asked me to go to the stores and get him a 'piece of chauff'. Again, I didn't understand Tony's cockney accent, and instead of feeling stupid to ask again what Tony wanted, I went straight to the stores and imitated Tony's cockney accent. I said, 'The foreman said to ask you for a piece of chauff', not having a clue what Tony meant. The next moment, the storeman gave me 'a piece of CHALK'. I felt a real fool and took the piece of 'chauff' to Tony, who said, 'Tha.' I didn't ask what 'Tha' meant but was getting to know some cockney words as I went along.

Whilst working on the assembly belt, I got friendly with another Anglo lad, Errol Evans, a tall, good-looking but shy sort of bloke, who worked in the turning section of Vickers. The salary with the turning department was a bit more than the assembly belt, so Errol got me interested to change to the engineering department as he would have a good word in for me with the foreman of the turning section. The foreman was very fond of Errol and treated him like a son. His name was Jim Guymer, so Jim took me on Errol's recommendation, and I left the assembly section.

Before I left the assembly section, I had approached Tony for an advance loan as I planned to get married. Tony asked me why I wanted such a large loan for. I said I wanted a big wedding with a big reception and invite all these Vickers Anglos to our wedding. Tony advised me not to be so foolish and said to me that fools only made feasts for wise men, and this time I understood his cockney accent and took his advice and hit the 'ammer on the 'ed.

Errol and I were getting along fine in the turning section, along with a machine setter operator called Curly Packer, who resembled one of the three stooges. 'Harpo', very white with curly ginger hair and rosy red cheeks. There was also a Polish progress chaser called Peter, whom Errol and I shared a lot of chats with during his checking our work as we talked about last night's TV or the latest news and gossip. There were a few English guys who by now at Vickers were getting a bit fed up with this sudden influx of Anglos. They didn't have to say they didn't approve of us, but you could see prejudice in their eyes as they looked at us full of hatred and muttered something under their breaths.

That was the way it was in the 1960s. Besides working at Vickers, I bumped into a bunch of English guys at one of the pubs. They were forming a rock 'n' roll group and were looking for a lead singer. We got talking, and finally, they agreed to try me out. When we met for rehearsal, I got along real fab with them, and they liked my style. We were getting ready for our first gig when suddenly, one of the boys of the group told me a shocking report that if his parents had found out that I was not English and from India, they weren't happy that their son had an Anglo Indian singer in their band.

That did it. I was gutted and shocked and didn't know what to say or do about it. I was very sad for a while, and it took me some time to get over this. That was my first taste of discrimination and was starting to remember Mr Sony from Kashmir's words: 'They will not like you in England and call you names, wogs go home, or Pakis or bloody foreigners'. How I wanted to go back and live like a king again, but it wasn't to be.

I even tried in desperation to enlist in the RAF and got through the test. I was willing to sign up for nine years. Zoe was gutted and told me not to be so foolish, that I was taking out my frustration of being refused by the band and their discrimination, but luckily for Zoe and me, I failed the medical at the RAF because of my hearing test and my past ear problems. So that was that regarding the band and the RAF.

Zoe and I were hopelessly in love and went about our young lives going to dances at the Locarno and the Orchid ballroom until one day we went to an Anglo Indian dance at the Stanley Halls, South Norwood. There was an Anglo band called the Starliners, who were pretty good but had a lead singer who was doing Elvis songs and not doing a very good job of it till finally, I plucked up enough courage to approach the band and asked if they didn't mind me doing a few songs with them. They agreed. I happened to go down a bomb with the band. The whole dance crowd kept asking for more and more, and of course, I was elated but felt sorry for their lead singer and didn't mean to make him feel small and dejected. How could I do this to my own countryman, but the guy congratulated me instead and offered me his job as well and said I deserved to take his place? I felt rotten to the core, but at least it was my first step with a band in the UK.

TREVOR 'ELVIS' TAYLOR

The Starliners consisted of Winston D'Cruz, the leader and drummer of the band; Kenny and Billy Baker on guitars and Doug Baker, their cousin, on bass guitar. We started rehearsals at Winston's flat in West Croydon, and we were getting on real fine and started doing regular gigs at the Star pub in West Croydon every Sunday night. I was starting to get popular with the Anglos and slowly getting quite famous. We started to get more dance gigs at Stanley Halls, also gigs at Middlesex, which had a huge following of Anglos.

Whilst in Middlesex, I bumped into another Anglo band, the 'Golden Oriels', which consisted of Johnny Bartel and his brothers Dave and Denzil and cousin Billy. Johnny the leader and keyboard player approached me and said he heard about my performances in Croydon. I was being talked about, this Elvis guy from Bombay who was gradually getting quite a name for himself. Johnny then proposed that I did a few gigs with them, whenever the Starliners could spare me. I agreed and started to do a few gigs with the 'Golden Oriels'. I started to get well known with them and started doing more gigs as we really jelled well together.

Until the big gig came along for us to perform at the Hammersmith Palais, we were the supporting band for the main star Billy Fury. We guys were a bit nervous at this big gig, so much so that when our turn came to perform, the revolving stage went round. The drummer, Billy, lost control of his bass pedal, and we started badly to a crowd of screaming teenagers who were only interested in Billy Fury, whom they came to see. We were an unknown group, but we put on a good show, and the teenagers had started to like us, but we were told to keep our act short as Billy Fury was the star of the show. I met Billy and also Desmond Decker in the green rooms before the show. Billy was a real friendly guy and had no hang-ups about being famous then.

Beginning of Trevor Elvis Taylor, with Ian Reece lead
guitar, Peter Arnold keys, Joe Phillips on vocals, me in
centre on mic and main vocals (All Shook Up)

Trevor 'Elvis' Taylor was now getting even more popular in the Anglo circuit, that more and more Anglo functions wanted me to perform as main guest artiste at Greenford Town Hall, Ruislip Town Hall and others. I can't remember keeping up, especially with organisers such as Claude Murdoch, Trevor Pearce and Wilbur Page. Wilbur started to have regular Anglo gigs at the Hammersmith Palais on Thursday nights, and I started to get more and more famous before I knew it. So now I was in a position to up my price for just an appearance of one spot at a Big Anglo dance and not flogging myself all night as the main singer and getting paid peanuts for it.

The biggest day of our lives,
Honey and I are finally hitched.

CHAPTER 13

OUR WEDDING

The date 16 December 1961 was the date set for our wedding. Was it a shotgun wedding? You could say that, but Zoe and I were inseparable and too much in love. She was only sweet 16, and I was 20. By the time we wed a year later, she was 17, and I was 21. She was pregnant with our firstborn son, Rudolph Aaron (Elvis's middle name, Aaron). It may have been a shotgun wedding, and I was not so keen on the idea at first as my brother Eddie said we wouldn't last. Zoe and I had more tiffs and makeups than anybody else, but I knew I couldn't last a day or two without Zoe, so we decided to tie the knot. It was a fairy tale wedding as her mum and sisters didn't approve of me as a rock 'n' roll singer and also the fights Zoe and I used to have through jealousy and stuff like that.

This, of course, brought shame on her mother and her sisters, who were starting to hate me for what I did, but that was the test of endurance and true love between Zoe and me. What God had meant for us to be together was destined for Zoe and me. Nothing else in the world mattered. Zoe was sweet and innocent, and I was this big bad boy from the ghettos of Bombay trying to be a decent husband and future father. Yes, the wedding finally took place on 16 December and has lasted fifty-five years till today, the year of 2017. Marvellous, eh, for those who thought we wouldn't last five minutes. We surprised the lot, didn't we? Today we have three lovely kids—Rudy, the eldest, with two sons and a daughter; Michelle, whom I saw been born at home with two sons and Nicky, the youngest, with two sons. In all, we have seven grandkids. I call them the Magnificent Seven. How about that then?

Before Rudy was born, Zoe and I had it real rough as we had rented an apartment in a basement bedsit at Clifton Road, South Norwood, SE 25, Zoe being pregnant. We were staying in our very own first place together in a bedsit which included a cooker, a dining table and a bed which converted to a sofa. We had to share the bathroom upstairs with the landlady and had to put in a shilling for the bath. This bedsit was sorted out by Zoe alone in her desperation for somewhere for us to own as our first home so to speak. She was determined to make our marriage work. As for me, I am ashamed to admit I didn't do anything towards it. She was my pillar of strength, and to this day, she still is. She made me realise a lot from her persistence and strength that anything was possible if you persisted. She definitely was an angel sent by God to save a wretched sinner like me and to change the type of person I was to finally realise my responsibilities and to love each other in sickness or in health, for richer or poorer.

Whilst at Clifton Road, Zoe, in her persistence, found us flat at Beulah Road, Thornton Heath, Surrey, which was a huge flat with separate kitchen/dining room, our own bathroom and a spare bedroom, which we rented to my brother Eddie and a huge living room which had our double bed in it. This was like a palace compared with the basement bedsit at Clifton Road, which we got slung out. As soon as the landlady found out Zoe was having a baby, Zoe didn't tell her she was expecting, or we wouldn't have got the bedsit. We were now a little better off and starting to live a bit more decently, what with our paraffin heaters and wild parties.

RUDY, our firstborn son, born 13 May 1962

Rudy's birth was something that was like a bolt of lightning that hit me out of the blue. I was so naive and didn't have a clue about childbirth.

When Rudy was first coming into this world, I didn't know what hit me as Zoe was in labour. I thought she was just having a bad stomach ache as she was getting real restless and started kicking about the bed in the early hours of the morning, so I woke Eddie, my brother, and asked him what he thought was wrong with Zoe, and he being the elder brother advised me that he thought she was about to give birth and that I should run down the road to the phone booth and call 999, which I did. When the ambulance crew finally arrived, Zoe was nearly giving birth. The ambulance crew took her away and asked if I wanted to come along too. I said it was OK as I didn't know whether I should go with her. I was such a green horn.

The next day was Sunday, and when I got to St Mary's Church, where Zoe and I married, I met Zoe's mum, and she asked me where is Zoe? I said Zoe had been taken in to Mayday Hospital to have her baby. Her mum then said to me, 'What did Zoe have?' I said I didn't know, and she said, 'Why don't you ring the hospital and find out?' so I did. I finally went to the hospital to see my firstborn son, Rudy. What an idiot I was. I cannot believe I was so naive.

Zoe's eighteenth birthday ended up with a bottle fight with me cracking a beer bottle on the head of Lance Dellows, a notorious streetfighter who started flirting with Zoe, who had now recently given birth to our firstborn son, Rudy. A year when Rudy was one year old, my brother Jimmy landed up at our place in a taxi all the way from Southampton and demanded that we pay the fare as he didn't have a cent. We somehow managed to scrape up £60 cash and paid the taxi fare. Now Jimmy, Colin Downs and Eddie my brother were still single and used to go boozing to the local pubs and were having fun bringing all sorts of girlfriends for rave ups at our flat, and it was getting a bit too much for Zoe and I to cope with especially with our newborn son, the wild parties and smoking pot and boozing.

Zoe and I decided it was time for us to move on to another flat, although we were helped with the rent from my brother Eddie, who later on moved and gave his room to another lodger we took on, Trevor McCabe. Trevor and I bought cycles from the cycle shop below on hire purchase. Me being married with a son stood guarantor for Trevor's payments if he defaulted, which he did, and I ended up paying for two bikes. Trevor disappeared from the face of the earth, and to this day, we don't know where he is. He used to give Zoe his dirty laundry and a little extra money to help buy some wool for the baby. Zoe had to use the laundrette down the road. We didn't have a telephone, so when we had to make our phone calls, we had to use the phone booth down the road. It was one with press button A or button B, which was owned and maintained by the GPO in those days.

Zoe and I finally moved from Beulah Road to another flat at Prince Road, South Norwood SE 25. This time it was an attic flat above another flat below us. The guy who lived below us would bang on his ceiling because our Rudy was crawling and thumping the floor nosily as he crawled. The bloke below us used to thump his ceiling with a broomstick and shout at the top of his voice, 'What have you got up there, elephants?' We were forced to tie our Rudy to a chair so he couldn't get out and bang or make any noise on the floor. It broke our hearts to do so, so we considered moving – again.

188 MOFFAT ROAD

We didn't last very long at 21 Prince Road as our fairy godmother, Melda, came to our rescue and this time arranged for us to rent a whole three-bedroom house, which her sister and husband rented and were moving on to Wales, as God was looking after us and guided Melda to help us with our first-ever three-bedroom semi with an upstairs and a downstairs, our own garden, separate kitchen, dining room, separate living room, bathroom with our own bathtub, gas cooker, oven and grill. Boy, we were in heaven. We were spoilt for space that I used to shout out to Zoe 'Where are you?' Rudy now had all the freedom to crawl and started learning to take his first steps. Oh, how we thanked Melda and the Lord Jesus for sending her to us. It was the start of our first decent home.

"The DIY Man about the House"

Now that we finally were on our first steps to owning our own property, I had to learn a few things about home maintenance, learn how to fix the necessary repairs around the house, and for a start, I had to fix us some wardrobes, so I got myself some Louvre doors to cover an alcove and some hinges with hanging rails and shelves. Don't ask me how I did it, but I can't remember how I did. It was a start.

We had the old type of sash cord windows that slides up and down and were in a very poor state, so I eventually agreed to have a chippy to change them for 'picture windows' it was the style that was then in the year 1963, with Louvre openings on the tops, we were now living in our posh house with our new picture windows and wardrobes, all this cost us just £4.50 a week in rent to the landlady and landlord who were an old couple that ran a hardware store in Croydon and sold paraffin, wood and other hardware. Zoe used to go there weekly to pay the rent and the old landlady used to feel sorry for Zoe a young mum with Rudy in his pram and would give Zoe back a ten bob note, which was worth half a quid to buy some sweets or goodies for her and young Rudy.

OUR FIRST STEP UP THE LADDER

The landlady liked Zoe and me and was like a fairy godmother to us that finally after renting for three years and now we had Michelle, our first daughter two years after Rudy, the old lady made us an offer to buy the house and make it our own. We were dumbstruck and told her that we just about managed to pay the rent and could in no way afford the selling price of £3,000. She then told us she would set up a private sale between her and us, that we'd still pay £4.50 a week or more if possible to clear the debt and fixed a solicitor to make the purchase legal at no extra charges. This was the first step up the ladder. We were very excited with the idea of owning our very own property. We started to work more hours at our jobs, especially Zoe (my pillar of strength), who started taking cleaning jobs for extra money and me as Trevor Elvis getting a few extra quid to help out, with a bit of overtime. We were slowly starting to climb that ladder.

I was totally useless at DIY jobs around the house, especially gardening, so with a little help from my neighbour, I had absolutely no idea of being a handyman around the house. My English neighbour Boyd, who was about ten years my senior, gave me a lot of tips and even lent me a few tools until I later on got my own. I had no idea of the use of hammers or chisels or anything of the sort and attempted to repair a broken kitchen window and ended up fixing the window opening towards inside instead of out and left it that way till the day came to sell this house. When the estate agent came to view, he remarked on my inside opening window and said, 'That's unusual, an inside opening window?' I learnt to do a lot of handy jobs the hard way.

Then I'll never forget the time at Moffat Road when at first, we were using paraffin heaters to warm ourselves and finally became a bit better off. We could afford to change to central heating, which was 'night storage radiators'. We had agreed to have them installed by two Irish electricians, but we had already fitted our lovely new green carpets. We then thought up a brilliant idea of how not to spoil the look of our new carpets by lifting them very carefully. We did so by lifting the end tacks to the carpets and lifted a few floorboards and passed the electric cable through, attached to the (wait for it) collar of our dear *cat*. We then went to the other end of this room, which was near the electric meter connections in a cupboard, and shook the cat food box and rattled it, shouting out, 'Kitty, kitty!' and there was the cat with the required electric cable attached to her collar, which was required by the electricians for the job to connect to our new night 'storage radiators'. We would now be the proud owners of 'central heating' and goodbye to good old paraffin heaters.

Zoe, Rudy and me were without a car, and we were living on the death walk as we called it and had to walk about half a mile down to the shops with Rudy in the pram to Thornton Heath High Street with friendly butchers, bakers, Tesco etc., until one day our Rudy was accidentally knocked down by a car at the pedestrian crossing as he let go off our hands, and he ran across as he was now a toddler and did not want to sit in the pram. The motorist immediately stopped and ran out of his car to help, and the friendly butcher also left his shop and ran over and carried our Rudy up in his arms as Zoe and I were in total shock. That was how it was back in 1961. Although we were foreigners, we felt there was some really decent English about who had decent feelings towards humanity. By the grace of God, our Rudy was all right, and we prayed and thanked God for saving our Rudy, whom we thought had nine lives as later on as he grew up, he had several accidents but was always protected by a divine power.

Michelle Elizabeth (Our First Daughter)

Michelle, our first daughter, was born on 5 August 1964, at home as Zoe and I decided, with the help of a local midwife, and boy was she a bit of an old battleaxe of a midwife as she bossed me about, shouting out orders on what my duties were to assist her. There I was, running up and down the stairs with supplies of hot water and towels. The old battleaxe warning me not to pass out on her, or if I did, she'd just step over me and continue without me.

That was a day I could never forget. The sight of my first daughter coming into this world and out of the womb brought tears to my eyes and a feeling I'll never forget, that for the first time in my life, I was beginning to feel like a real father, the feeling I never experienced with our Rudy. I was too naive and inexperienced and stupid, but now after the birth of Michelle, I was starting to grow up and realise I was now a father of two kids. Getting rid of the afterbirth was an experience never to be forgotten as from instructions from the battleaxe and how I had to burn the afterbirth in my garden. The nightmares I had over it were to last a lifetime that made me feel sick to this very day, so I'll skip the details, if you don't mind.

Michelle aged 5 years

CHAPTER 14

TREVOR TAYLOR, THE GREASE MONKEY

The birth of Michelle was a blessing in disguise because we were given a grant towards the new baby's layette and things. It was £15, and in 1964, it was worth quite a bit and enabled me to put it towards buying my very first car or van that was available at the time with a little help from my friend, an Anglo Indian guy named George White, whom I met up with as he lived a few blocks away from me. George worked at a garage servicing cars as a so-called mechanic and had a glass eye and poor vision. He was about ten years older than me. He used to come round our place and loved singing and dancing, so we clicked. He also had a good sense of humour and was very kind with our two kids and used to spend a lot of time with us. He even helped us with domestic chores around the house.

Then one day he asked me if I was interested in working at his garage as a mechanic's aid, greasing up cars that came for servicing. He would speak to the foreman and put in a good word for me. I took up George's offer and started work as a lubrication bay operator (a grease monkey), and of course we, had another Anglo Indian mate working in the stores who got us any motor parts that was required, no questions asked. George suggested it was time to buy my own car/van that was going cheap for £15, so the baby's layette money came in handy, and George and I got this green Fordson van for £15.

During the lunch hour breaks at the garage where we worked, George took it upon himself to teach me to drive around the forecourt of the garage with different cars of customers that came in for servicing. They were a lot better cars than my old heap of a van. George would sit as a co-passenger and give me instructions on driving and changing gears and clutch control, etc., but then George got a ballocking for using the customers' cars to teach me. I was going round and round the forecourt with George and me and the Scottish foreman running after us and asking us to stop at once. If that was bad, we got worse by George guiding me to drive the customers' cars onto the ramp, which required quite a bit of skill to aim for the ramps that had a pit below to service cars. I was getting the hang of it until I heard the loud Scottish foreman yelling out at George to stop me driving the customers' cars onto the ramps, but old George and I just did what we wanted to do, and that was that.

George started to give me driving lessons. The only snag was with the three forward gears of my van. The second gear used to slip out of gear as the cogs were worn out. You had to hold onto the gearstick so as not to let it slip out of gear. If you didn't hold on to the gearstick, it would jump out of gear, and the gearstick, being quite a large one about two feet long with a black knob to hold onto, would jump out with quite some force and whack you on your knee, especially if you were the passenger, and when I did forget to hold onto it, poor George would get a wallop quite often, and so this carried on for quite some time till I finally got used to it. Then after a few weeks' training, George suggested I apply for a driving test. Wow, was I excited.

To prepare my van for the driving test, according to George, my van was in perfect condition apart from a few adjustments such as adding a pair of direction indicators; otherwise, I had to give hand signals. George fitted a pair of flashing indicators with the compliments of his store man from the garage and together with rubber tubing to hold a glass window on either side of the van. He had to cut the metal sides of the van to fit the windows on either end and with the new flashing indicators fitted above each window onto the roof edges of the van. To finish off the back of the van, George managed to get hold of some decent red carpets for the rear of the van as it had no seats at the back. The colour of the van was dark green with a pair of massive headlights on either end of the bonnet. The bonnet had a flapped opening hinges on either end to get to the engine and had a pair of doors at the back for passengers, so we painted the headlights a smart black and polished up the chrome work, and I was finally ready to take the driving test.

I arrived at the driving test centre full of confidence with George as my co-driver and George reminding me not to forget to hold on to the dodgy gearstick, so I walked in to meet the examiner who was to become a 'terminator' with my dodgy gearstick, which I nervously forgot to hold onto several times during the test. The examiner didn't look very happy and asked me to pull up in frustration, which I did quite sharply, bringing the van to a sudden halt as I presumed he meant to stop in an emergency, so I did. The examiner looked quite red-faced and cross. I said, 'What is the problem?' And he said very plainly, 'You've FAILED', in quite a sharp tone of voice. I replied, 'WHY?' and he replied with a sigh that I'd failed on several points, the main one being holding onto the gearstick with one hand and the other hand onto the steering wheel and then letting go of the steering wheel to turn on the indicators. To make matters worse, I was told by George during my driving lessons to depress the clutch pedal each time I did a left or right turn around bends and didn't know that would be like sailing along in neutral until the examiner pointed this to me.

I was devastated at the news of the failure and told George the bad news, and he said, 'Never mind, Trev, you can apply again. I applied twenty-five times and failed on the eye test bit, before you start the test' (as that's what the examiner asks you to read a number plate of a car twenty-five yards away). Poor George with his poor vision and his glass eye failed them all, even though he brought along his own measuring tape to measure the twenty-five yards as he doubted the examiner on each occasion. George turned to me and said 'You know what, Trev? It's our colour. We're not white.'

All this time, whilst I was being taught by George, I presumed he was a fully qualified driver and didn't know, or he didn't say he hadn't passed his test. He told me not to worry about it as he had got away with it for the last twenty-five years and did not bother with taking any more driving tests in the future.

On failing me, the examiner advised me to take professional driving lessons before I took any further test again and to get a more suitable vehicle that was a bit more roadworthy. I told George this, and he said, 'They do not realise what a decent vehicle you have. They are just jealous, just because you are coloured and own a posh van.'

I didn't bother to apply for another test for a year or so, and in the meantime, I had wheels to go shopping and avoid the 'death walk' of Moffat Road and was driving about quite happily with Rudy and Michelle at the back on my beautiful red carpets, with Zoe in front in the passenger seat with bruised knees, so much so that she got used to hold onto the gearstick at times when I'd forget. We'd go to visit my mum and Zoe's mum and show off my prized green van and sometimes even head down to the seaside such as Camber Sands, Hastings or Clacton, and I remember one time at Camber Sands, there was a traffic jam that was being controlled by a policeman urging the traffic to move on. Seeing the copper, I began to panic, and when the copper indicated to me, waving his arms hurriedly for me to proceed forward, I panicked and stalled the van several times, with this copper looking quite frustrated, saying, 'Come on, son, don't muck about. I haven't got all day.' That was how it was in 1963/64. Them Bobbies didn't bother you too much. You got away with a lot, or I was just plain lucky.

Trevor 'Elvis' Taylor,

POSTMAN!

I am now a family man with two kids and a wife to support with a meagre income to live on.

I was forced to find work, apart from depending on earning enough from being a full-time entertainer.

In the meantime, I found out that there were vacancies for postmen in the Thornton Heath area, so I applied, and before you could say Jack, I got the job, which was down the road for me, but the only snag was I had to start work at 5 a.m. Wow! I got kitted out with my Royal Mail outfit with dark blue woollen jacket and trousers, a hat with a Royal Mail badge and my name and number on another badge on my lapel; I looked like an airline pilot and was quite proud of myself.

George Chapman was my instructor for the first two weeks of my training for my postal delivery round. He showed me how to learn sorting, and I had to pass a sorting test, which I did quite easily, and then was put on a proper postal round, which was the 'Leander Road' round, and I was given a royal blue sack to put in my prepared mail in bundles to deliver from house to house. I got bus fares to and from my starting point of my round and back to the sorting office. My duty finished around midday after doing a second delivery. After the first delivery, which I left the office around 7 a.m. and was back to the office around 10 a.m., I was so hungry I could eat a horse. I used to stop at the butchers, who did fresh hot steak and kidney pies which I devoured with a lovely cup of hot tea at the PO canteen. Oh, and there was also a cup of tea at 6.30 a.m. before you left for your round, which we chipped in some money for the tea maker. Derek Rodgers was the chief tea maker and used to shout 'Tea up!' and we would all rush for our morning cuppa.

One of the postmen was a guy, Dave Jennings, who resembled the actor Robert Mitcham and had a Spanish wife; therefore, he became my friend. He also was the postman who delivered to my house on Moffat Road, and Dave and me got along very well at the sorting office and used to have a lot of banter there, especially with George, my instructor, who used to welcome me every morning and say to me, 'Hello, me ol' garlic', because he thought I reeked of garlic, which used to wind me up a lot as everyone else in the office would have a laugh at me. I would try to ignore it, and then suddenly, I would attack George with a reply as 'Did you smell your mouth this morning? I just thought I smelt shit', and the rest of the posties would have a laugh.

This banter carried on every day, but somehow I kinda liked George, who reminded me of my father a bit. I had a lot of fun in the PO with a lot of banter during preparation for deliveries and, of course, the fresh air, and all that walking kept me fit, and well, Trevor Elvis was now a 'postie' singing 'Return to Sender' on his rounds.

In the meantime, I managed to flog off my much treasured green van, which I did in a part exchange with a car dealer for a Ford Esquire Estate car with everything in working order, including the gear lever that didn't jump out and whack you on your kneecaps and proper direction indicators and wing mirrors. At last, I've got myself a decent motor, and now I could get some proper driving lessons with a proper driving instructor, which I did. Even though the lessons were a bit expensive, I managed a few lessons to brush me up for the driving test, and guess what, I passed with flying colours after months of driving the old green banger without a full licence, no insurance or road tax. I got away with murder. Today they would probably lock me up or throw the book at me. George White was really happy I'd passed the driving test. I'll never know if he ever passed his driving test. He never did mention it again.

After a few months as a walking postie, I decided to apply for the post of postman/driver, which required a postal van driving test. I passed the PO driving test and was ready for the post as postman/driver, only to be told there were no vacancies at Thornton Heath and that I would have to report to the South Croydon branch, which I did after two weeks of my holiday due to me.

Having passed my driving test, I was ecstatic and immediately planned to drive off to Spain on a camping holiday, so I mustered up some info from the RAC with route maps, etc. and started to put my holiday plan into motion.

My Ford Escort (I drove to Spain with it 3000 miles)

My new Baby VW Polo Beats I have today.

My Triumph Herald. Outside 188 Moffat Road 1960's

My first bike BSA Bantam

CHAPTER 15

OUR FIRST FAMILY HOLIDAY
CAMPING IN SPAIN

Before commencing on our first-ever holiday abroad with Rudy, 3 years old, and Michelle, 18 months, the year 1965, we ventured out with my emergency breakdown kit with a little help from my friend Rudy Barraclouch, who worked for Dees motors, and let me have the breakdown kit for free and warned me to take care as my new motor had just three forward gears and one reverse and that I'd have problems going uphill on the mountainous roads through France into Spain and doubted I'd make it back. I told him I was confident of my 'new motor', and I'd make it anywhere in the world. He just laughed and told me I was crazy, which I probably was to venture out on this 3,000-mile round trip.

Zoe, Rudy, Michelle and me set out with our full camping gear to Spain complete with a five-gallon spare can of petrol in the luggage compartment as we were told petrol was very expensive in France, with our supplies of tinned canned baked beans, curry powders and supplies. The camping gear on top of our roof rack, we were off to Dover to board the ferry boat to Calais in France. When we landed in France, I was faced with driving now on the other side of the road. In England, with the road manners, stopping for pedestrians and hand signals to slow down, I nearly got my hand chopped off with French drivers whizzing past me left and right.

With my right-hand drive car and my GB stickers, I was constantly honked, and after a while, I got used to it, especially when I had to overtake from the left instead of the right. It was a nightmare, but by the grace of God, who has always protected me from a little boy, we were always safe in his hands. I guess he always protected his once altar and choir boy.

We drove through France past the mad traffic at the famous Arc de Triumph and got through somehow until we were so tired and hungry. We stopped to buy some grub. We ended up with a full roasted chicken and ate it like starving animals and tore it to bits with our fingers, and boy was it good followed with a drink of Coke and a few good fags. We were quite refreshed and carried on to find our first camping site in France. We drove on and on till we finally found a camping site and started to pitch our tent and unloaded our supplies. We were so tired we all slept like babies and woke up bright and refreshed for our first morning in France with our cold showers, coffee and breakfast cooked on our camping stove. We had a good feed. We were all set to carry on for our journey through the Pyrenees mountains of France, leading to the rough roads to Spain.

What with the oncoming traffic and especially the big trucks nearly pushing me over the mountain edges, it was a nightmare until we decided to pull up somewhere safe to park overnight in our car until the morning. We slept in the car the four of us and kept wondering if there were any wild animals such as mountain lions or anything of the kind. We said our prayers and dozed off to sleep and woke up at the crack of dawn. After a nice cup of coffee and some cornflakes, we carried on to Spain.

Spain was warm and friendly, and the Spanish folk took to us as if we were one of them, especially with our young kids. They were very fond of children, and the camping site's owner took a liking to our little Michelle and offered us a few extra privileges such as hot milk and some fresh Spanish food. We set up tent for a few days at the Costa Brava and were settling down for our first night under the

Spanish stars. We woke up and started our breakfast with our eggs and bacon and baked beans, sausages and curried tomato and onion fry up. We had the rest of the campers who were either Dutch or Germans who were attracted by the smell of our curries and gathered round our tent to sample some of our delicious breakfast, which we willingly shared with these Dutch burly guys. They, in turn, brought in some of their grub to share with us. These Dutch guys as I later discovered were Dutch policemen on holiday and took a liking to us. Later on, they asked us to join them on our first night out to a Spanish nightclub that had flamenco dancers and champagne. We agreed to go, after the camping site kind lady agreed to look after our kids.

The nightclub was a really lively joint with champagne and a meal included and then the flamenco dancers whom I tried to photograph. I drank quite a bit of champagne. It tasted like lemonade as I thought, only to discover the flamenco dancers seemed to double in numbers and seemed out of focus in my camera. That was when I finally passed out and realised the next morning that I had to be carried to the camping site by one of the burly Dutch cops like a sack of potatoes and was flung into my tent to sleep it off. I awoke with a throbbing headache, and it was relayed about my condition of the previous night. I thanked them for their assistance and asked them to join us for breakfast.

One of the great sights not to be missed was the famous bullfight, which we saw in the city of Barcelona, all that killing and blood all over the place. It was ghastly and cruel. Then the next thing I always wanted to do was drive along the sands on the beach, like I've seen it done in the movies, so we ventured on to the beach with our two kids, Zoe and me. I was having a ball driving along the sandy beach until I came upon a mound of sand and tried to drive over it, only to find my rear wheels caught in a spin, and the more I revved, the worse it got until a bunch of Spanish guys came to help us out of this mess. By now, the car was almost tilting over to one side.

The kids and Zoe got out with me inside, following instructions from the Spanish guys, including a Spanish cop as well. They all pushed and managed to get me out of there eventually, and that was the last time I ever drove on any beach again. We enjoyed the rest of our camping trip, and the kids had a great time helping with the camping chores of fetching fresh water for cooking, although Michelle suffered a bit of heatstroke for a while. The camping Spanish lady was very kind in taking her into her villa for a bit of tender care for a day or two until she recovered.

At the end of two weeks, after doing a bit more touring, we were set to head off home, only to discover the engine of my car was smoking up, so I drove to a nearby garage to cool off the engine, and not realising the engine was still red-hot, I poured in fresh cool water into the radiator and discovered much later on that I'd done more damage to my engine by cracking the cylinder block and wondered why my engine oil looked a chalky grey in colour. I paid no attention to this and carried on with my 1,500 miles back to Calais to catch the ferry boat back to the UK.

Whilst on the ferry boat on our return, I discovered countless amounts of GB cars in quite a mess through accidents, and they had posher cars than mine, so I didn't feel that bad apart from my cracked cylinder block. Then we had another stroke of luck as one of the stewardess of the ferry felt sorry for us with our kids, and especially Michelle a sick baby, she offered us a comfortable spare cabin till the end of our return ferry journey. God was always protecting us, no matter what silly things we did. He was always there.

Back in the UK, I saw Rudy from Dees and told him I didn't need the breakdown kit after all. He just laughed and said, 'Thank God you are all back safe and sound.'

I got my engine fixed with a reconditioned one and then reported for duty at the South Croydon sorting office as a postman driver and enjoyed that for a few weeks. I couldn't get on with one of the inspectors who was giving me a hard time and overloading me with loads of extra parcel deliveries that I couldn't cope with, so I resigned and told him to stuff his job up his arse. That was the long and short of my PO van driver for now until much later, I joined the PO at East Croydon in the year 1969. I will explain about that later, until my next move.

TT the Potato Man

I was out of a job but not for long until I met a guy named Conrad Gomes, who was an ex-postal worker as well and was working as a driver delivering spuds at a potato firm. He said he could fix me up as a driver for those big potato lorries delivering spuds. Now this was a blessing in disguise as I needed the experience of driving big vehicles and getting used to driving with the use of wing mirrors. Conrad spoke to the boss of the firm, who decided to take me on because of Conrad's recommendation, so Conrad began to show me the ropes of how to handle this big ten-ton lorry, which I had no clue what to expect as it was completely different from the gears of a car, whereas you had to double declutch for every gear; otherwise, you'd get a crunching sound if you didn't, as was the case when I first got into the cab with Conrad as my co-driver and the boss of the firm asking Conrad, 'Are you sure this guy knows how to drive?' 'Yes, yes, Gov, he'll be OK with me in a minute or so,' said Con. 'He'd better be' was the reply. So Con and I went off down the road as I eventually got the hang of it, and so the Gov said to me, 'Eight o'clock Monday morning, you're on the Crawley round.' 'Yes, boss, I'll be there. Thanks for the job. See you, Con. Bye,' said me.

I was a bit fed up with the potato rounds, with the experience of driving heavier vehicles. I decided to apply for a job as a bus driver at London Transport. I then got called up for an interview. I was OK at the interview for the buses and told I was to take a driving test.

On the Buses (1966–1969)

Elvis was still in the British charts with the threat of the Beatles and Rolling Stones and all that crap that was nothing like the fifties rock 'n' roll.

I reported at the Chiswick training centre and was met by an elderly sergeant major sort of Scottish bloke, who was to be my trainer, and another black guy to be trained as bus driver as well, so we proceeded to our bus cabs.

I was told to drive along the Chiswick high street and around the block to see how I handled the bus. The steering wheel was about two feet in diameter and felt gigantic. I was rapped several times on my hands as I crossed steered, by my instructor as he was right behind me. He kept barking out orders in my ears like an old sergeant major, and every time I turned round to look at him, he yelled out even louder, 'Keep your eyes on the road, you clot! You're not driving in India now! You are in flipping London, you hear!' This went on and on until I turned round to give him a deadly stare as if I wanted to kill him, and he said, 'Do you want to chin me then? Let's see you try it.' I said, 'If I had to chin you, you wouldn't wake up', and with that, he gave a hearty laugh, and so did I.

When we arrived at the next bus garage for a break of tea and fags, he told me not to get myself worked up as his bark was worse than his bite. I think he sort of liked my spirit, and my driving was not so bad as the West Indian black guy, who was shouted out even louder than me. 'Come on, you jungle bunny! You're not driving in the jungle now!' The black guy didn't like it at all and said to me that the instructor was prejudiced against coloured people. I said that the instructor was just used to his sergeant major ways and didn't really mean what he said. I guess he had not long left the army, but the black guy just wasn't cut out to be a bus driver and eventually failed his test.

I was next taken onto the famous skid patch at the Chiswick training centre and was about to experience the fright of my life as I was told to drive on this wet and greasy ground round and round and building up my speeds to 40/45 MPH. Then the instructor would grab hold of the handbrake, and the bus went into a fantastic skid I've never seen before. I was told before hand to steer left if the bus was skidding to the left and keep pumping my brakes in jerks to gradually slow down the bus. My heart was in my mouth, but I eventually began to enjoy it. I was also instructed on how to brake gently so as to give my passengers a smooth ride and was trained to bring my foot down on the brakes as if it was a feather. I learnt fast, and with the result, I passed and was told to report to Brixton bus garage the next week with my much earned PSV (Public Service Vehicle licence). I felt ten feet tall.

The first week at Brixton garage, I was on route learning. I was put on the 133 route to Liverpool Street. What a joke that turned out to be the first time I went out with actual passengers on this double decker bus. I kept taking wrong turns down wrong routes, and the bus conductor, who was a big fat guy from Sri Lanka, was doing his nut and ringing the bell frantically for me to stop and guided me onto the proper route with all the passengers looking stunned. Then I made another clanger when I drove the 133 to Hendon. On returning from Hendon, I accidentally took a wrong turn and ended up onto the M1 motorway. The conductor kept ringing the bell frantically for me to stop. I then immediately stopped and realised I was on the motorway. What could I do? I couldn't drive to the next exit to turn back as it would be too far, so the conductor said he'd stop the traffic to enable me to do a three-point turn on this motorway and then get back to my proper route. Luckily, it was Sunday, and there was not much traffic about, so we got away with it.

There were several other incidents, but the one I'll never forget is when I drove the 95 bus to Cannon Street Station. On my return journey, it was simply pouring down with rain, and the traffic lights near Cannon Street bridge was out of order. There was a traffic cop guiding the traffic in the pouring rain. He didn't look very happy. When he saw my bus waiting, he beckoned me, waving frantically to get a move-on, so I didn't hesitate and put my foot down on the accelerator, and as I was gaining some speed, suddenly, a big HGV lorry cut in from the left in front of my bus, forcing me to hit the brakes, and in doing so, I got into the most horrific skid. The bus swayed from left to right and right to left, just about missing the traffic cop, who ran off the road for shelter. By now, all my skid patch training went out of the window, but I somehow managed to control the bus a bit by pumping the brakes and tried to go with the skid, but the gradient in the road was sloping downwards, and there was not much else I could do apart from ramming into a few cars, and especially this car, a sports MG Midget, whose driver I remember had his hands covering his face downwards to protect himself. I then rammed into him. The bus then stopped just a few feet away to stop my bus going over the bridge.

My heart was in my mouth, and I was shaking like a leaf. The copper by now came up to me and said he'd witnessed how the lorry had cut in from the left and didn't stop. He was the cause of this whole accident. He said that when I felt comfortable enough to drive my bus away from the scene, I should do so. I told the cop that I was not in a state to drive, and he told me that if I didn't drive now, it would affect my nerves and that I'd probably never drive again. He said, 'Relax yourself and have a nice cup of tea and a fag to settle your nerves and then get on with it', so I did just that and drove the partly damaged bus back to the bus depot at Brixton.

The duty times were crazy. I had to get up at 4 a.m. at some weeks for the early shifts and sometimes drive the all night runs. The shifts were killing my health, and I was skinny as a rake and had no time for proper meals and had to do with cold food from the vending machines at the bus garages. Zoe was getting worried about my health, so she found out about some pick-me-up tonic called Biostrath, a Swedish tonic that seemed to do the trick, and within a short while, I was starting to improve my appetite and haven't stopped since. The job used to get me down with so many stops and starts with the bell constantly ringing to stop or start by the bus conductor, and the driving became a chore as it was no joy driving. The sooner you began driving, you had to stop either at request stops or for heavy traffic or traffic lights. It began to get me down, so much so that I'd decided to just drive past all the stops and not bother picking up any more passengers. Almost every day I had to report to the garage manager for some complaint or the other, so much so I decided I had had enough of this boring job.

I met an Anglo Indian friend, Mervin Lissenburg, who told me about this lovely job at the post office at East Croydon sorting office as there were a lot of us Anglos working there, and the wages were good, so at once, I applied. Very soon, I was called for a PO test and shortly after joined the training school at East Croydon. I had to pass a sorting test. As I was an ex-postal worker, I managed the test quite easily and had to start work as a walking postman in the year 1969 until 1989, the year I eventually got medically retired from the PO.

BACK TO THE PO

A total of twenty glorious years at East Croydon were the best years of my life as the company of postal workers was fantastic. It was like being in school again among naughty boys having fun and teasing one another all the time and the PO inspectors scolding us as little children as we treated the workplace like a playground. Although we had to start work at 5 a.m., we were bright and breezy at that hour as there was constant banter and Mickey taking, and you'd never had to get angry or lose it as you would get a bad name, so you had to give as good you got.

I started on a postal round in New Addington and had to deliver letters on the Dunley Drive estate and had to walk from door to door, pushing mail through letter boxes in the rain or snow, feeling a bit fed up at times. When I got fed up with delivering letters in the rain, one day a lady came out of her house and accused me of putting wet mail through her letter box. I apologised and said that I couldn't help it, but she got stroppy with me and said she was going to report me, so I said to her, 'You can do just that.' I was then called into the office and was reprimanded about the complaint. I said to myself, 'Right, I'll show this bitch a thing or two. She doesn't know who she is dealing with.' The next time I passed her house on a rainy day, I made sure her letter got well soaked, and to make matters worse, I held her letters under a leaking drainpipe and shoved the soggy mail into her letterbox. I never heard anymore from the bitch again. I could be real nasty with people like that. They deserved to be tuned up by me.

Despite it all, I enjoyed the lovely fresh mornings, and the healthy walking kept me in a fit condition, so much so when I returned to the PO, I used to tuck into a healthy breakfast after my first delivery at the PO canteen, with eggs and bacon, sausages, fried toasts, baked beans and tomatoes and two or three cups of tea and a grand fag for afters.

Boy those were the days. That was about 10 a.m. and 11 a.m. We would have to deliver our second round called the B delivery and were out of the office like a shot as we wanted to finish the B delivery and get home ASAP and have the afternoon either at home or back to the office for overtime. This went on for about a couple of months until I got the urge to apply for a postman driver's job, and very soon, I was given a duty driving the minibus and dropping off postmen at their delivery points, and this job was a doddle. I was even happier.

Michelle as a baby and Rudy aged about three.

Michelle, Nicky (Centre) and Rudy,
& my old Triumph Herald.

Nicola Jean our second daughter (Nicky the rebel) at her christening and
Zoe, Rudy & Michelle, Outside 188 Moffat Road, Thornton Heath, Surrey.

EAR PROBLEMS WORSENING

Now as I was quite happy in the PO, I was suffering with my ear problems and found out that I was losing my hearing, so the specialist at Mayday Hospital recommended I should try wearing a hearing aid, and immediately, I said no way as imagine the way I'd look with this thing popping out of my ear. The doctor said I'd get used to it, but I refused, although I took the hearing aid to try out and see how I'd get on. In the meantime, one of my ears developed an infection of mastoid and had to be operated, and after the operation, my hearing had got worse.

I was now forced to wear the hearing aid, which wearing it at the PO was in a joke itself as I had no end of Mickey taking as I was this Elvis with a hearing aid. I had to put up with all the banter. I used to take out my hearing aid at times when sounds got too loud for me. and I remember the time when I had delivered the van to the South Croydon PO and had to be picked up by another driver back to our office to go home. This other driver said he heard a whistling sound coming out of the engine as this van had its engine inside the van, so as I leaned forward to listen to this 'whistling' sound, the driver then said that the sound had got louder. As I leaned back, he said the sound got fainter, and immediately, I suspected that it might be my hearing aid, might have gone off whilst in my pocket and therefore whistling. Very carefully, I managed to turn the aid off, and immediately doing so, the whistling stopped. The driver said, 'It's stopped.' I said, 'Wow, what was it?' Pretending that I didn't have a clue, he said, 'Never mind. Whatever it was, it's gone now. At least I don't have to ring up for the breakdown.'

That was one of my hearing aid experiences until another time I had locked myself out of my van by mistake and was really worried as the keys were inside the van, and I needed help. Until this other van driver named Adrian pulled up and offered to help me get my keys out of the locked van and said that if I bent down a bit, he'd climb on my back to stretch out and try to reach for the van keys through a narrow gap of the van window, and then he somehow managed to get the van keys out and told me to lower him down. I, of course, didn't hear him telling me to lower him down until he shouted, 'Lower me down, you deaf dog!' Again, I was grateful he got me out of trouble and took no offence of his unkind remarks.

The year was the late '60s, about 1968, and Elvis was doing a special comeback TV special as he was beginning to lose his fame a bit with the Beatles and Stones, etc. We still had a black-and-white TV and was quite happy watching Elvis in his black leather outfit and belting out all his favourites that to this very day are still going strong. I was still doing a few gigs with stand-in band guys until I decided to form a proper group of my own with a few Anglo musicians and started getting a few gigs at pubs and social clubs, etc., until my ears again started playing up, and I had to see the ear specialist again, and this time the specialist enquired, 'Which ear seems to be the problem?' I replied, 'Since 1968.' The doctor then said, 'I mean which ear, left or right!' I saw the funny side and just laughed, but the doctor didn't. I was really struggling with my ears, and my hearing was getting from bad to worse and was really beginning to be the DEAF OF ELVIS as this deaf Elvis from India and all that fame and fortune left behind and now struggling as a postman driver in the UK. What would my boss in India think of me now?

PUTTING UP WITH MY DEAFNESS?

Although I was now more deaf and getting worse, I began to feel depressed at times, especially when in conversations. Some people would be very unkind. If I asked them to repeat what they had said, they would say, 'Oh, never mind.' They would not realise how they were hurting a deaf person like me or any other deaf person. Because of my sometimes cheerful personality as an entertainer, I would cheer myself up again.

CHAPTER 16

NICOLA JEAN (OUR SECOND DAUGHTER, THE REBEL)

I managed to somehow be happy working like a dog all those hours overtime at the PO, sometimes from 5 a.m. till 8 p.m., to earn a decent living. With Zoe working and our joint wages, we were just about managing until our third child.

The day Nicky, as we named her, was our second daughter, she was two weeks overdue, giving Zoe a hard time. When the day finally arrived, I followed the ambulance to the hospital. She didn't give Zoe any trouble with her birth at the hospital as the nurses had told Zoe that the baby wasn't due for some time, and she should relax, but Zoe said she felt the baby coming out, and they said to her, 'Don't be silly, you've had two children before, and you should know better.' With that, Zoe then gave one hell of a scream, and the baby's head was halfway out. She had all these nurses and doctors running all over the place in an emergency to deliver Nicky.

What will we name the baby was the next question. We were expecting a baby boy. I had the name of Nicky for a boy called Nicolas, and during this time of deciding of what to name this baby girl instead, I suddenly thought the Hindi word in India for eventually coming out was 'Nical guyya', so I thought Nicky would suit Nical guyya as she'd finally come out after much difficulty.

Niki as she is called today, The Rebel Rouser.

Zoe
The WONDER WOMAN!

No Time for Tears

Let me tell you about my pillar of strength, super mum, wife and best friend. I wouldn't be here alive today if it wasn't for her and her tenacity. It all started way back when we married and lived in different flats and struggled with our kids, with Zoe taking our kids to baby minders so she could work to help out with managing the finances, and it was a heartbreaking experience leaving her kids and hurrying off to work. There was no time for tears.

When the going got tough, there was Zoe who fought it even harder to achieve her goal no matter what, leaving her kids and putting up with the shit at shitty jobs and leave her kids crying at the babysitters. There was no time for tears. She was tough, and till today she was and will always be a tough fighter. She always had the mother of our Lord Jesus Christ on her side, who always protected her.

OUR WAY BACK TO JESUS

Zoe had always as a kid had a deep faith in Our Blessed Virgin Mary the Mother of Our Lord and Saviour Jesus Christ, and with her deep faith, she always seemed to get out of her problems, with a little help from Our Lady, and to this day, she always depends on Our Lady. She never lets Zoe down.

As for me, an ex-choir boy and altar boy, I also had this deep faith that Jesus loved me as a little boy, loves and watches over Zoe, our family and me.

Although for a while, we stopped attending Mass on Sundays as we should and tried keeping the Ten Commandments. We did go astray because we as Catholics were now practicing birth control, and when we went to confess our sins of birth control, the priest was not in favour of it and refused to give us absolution. We then stopped going to church for a while until we went to another kinder priest, who understood the difficulties of having a large family, and then he agreed to give us absolution, that we should go according to our conscience. We took his advice, and after that, we started attending Sunday Mass again and received Holy Communion. Our faith was renewed, and we were trying to be Catholics again and set an example to our three kids. Things started to get better as our faith grew stronger.

Our Lord and Saviour Jesus Christ.

MALTA (OUR FIRST HOTEL HOLIDAY)

Zoe was now well established at Wakefield Fortune and back to work after having our baby Nicky that she was offered a free holiday to Malta, and it turned out to be simply the best holiday yet. This hotel in Comino, Malta, was something we'd never experienced before. It was like paradise. We had this whole little island to ourselves, and from the moment we landed, we were treated like VIPs because we met this 'captain' of the ferry boat, who was going to get us to the island of Comino. This captain's name was Peter.

We never understood why Peter was ignoring us and letting all the other English tourists into the boat before us and kept signalling us to wait until all passengers were in and seated at the rear of the boat. I was wondering where Peter was going to put us, but when he invited us to board his boat eventually, I realised he had a special place for us in his 'captain's' cabin.

I realised then that he'd taken a shine to us from then on and started to give us special treatment. He treated us like we were his own family, maybe because we weren't white as the Maltese are quite brown like us and perhaps thought we reminded him of his own family. Peter could not do enough for us as he helped us with our luggage to this beautiful hotel, the one and only hotel on this island of Comino with no traffic and not a single car and completely cut off from civilisation. We were put up in style of five-star rating with all meals included and with fresh towels and bedding changed every day. We were in paradise surrounded by this blue-green sea and a beach of our very own as nobody else could use our beach but us hotel residents, which was about twelve in all, but only on weekends, there were tourists who came to invade our island for a few hours, which was quite tolerable.

One of the special nights was a special barbecue night for the hotel guests, and a band of musicians were brought in to entertain us, and of course, Trevor Elvis got very excited about the band coming in and decided to do a turn with the band boys, which turned out with everyone rockin' and rollin' the night away, and then Peter the ferry boatman, getting very drunk and excited that his newfound 'family' whose dad was a bit of an Elvis, jumped on the stage bare chest, in his shorts and, pretty pissed, grabbed hold of the mic and shouted out to the crowd that my family and I were his special family from England. By the grace of God, we had a lovely two weeks and returned safe and sound.

Chapter 17

Elvis the King Is Dead!

One of the photo shoots by my daughter Niki.

One of many costumes at the start of my Rockin' Days

I carried on quite disappointedly, for a while bumming around with a few other bands and was getting nowhere, until I decided to take my family on a short holiday to the Lake District, which was in August 1977. We left at the beginning of August, when the kids broke up for their summer hols, and we had a lovely break for two weeks. Until we returned on 16 August 1977, when I turned on the TV and the newscaster announced the most disheartening news I'd ever heard, 'Elvis Presley the king is dead', I was numb with shock. I couldn't find the strength to call out to Zoe and tell her what I'd just heard. We were all in total shock and so was the rest of the world. How could he die, so soon at the age of 42? How dare he die on us Anglos who adored him and millions of fans all over the world? He never even stepped ashore in the UK or any other part of the world either to all those millions who wanted to see him live, We'd only seem him in movies but never in the flesh. How could he do this to us and especially me, Trevor Elvis? He was like a brother to me, and I truly loved him. I cried and cried for days and weeks. I lost a dear friend, and part of me was dying too, this poor boy from the ghettos of Bombay, now in the UK, and with hope that someday I would finally get to see and meet my king.

A year later, 1978

Elvis the musical was a West End play in London and were auditioning for Elvis lookalikes, sound likes, which got me interested, so I applied at the Regent's theatre run by Ray Cooney. When I arrived at the audition, there were thousands of applicants, and I thought that this was not a good idea, but I finally plucked up enough courage and went for it with my bro-in-law, Joe, to back me up on guitar. The auditions started off with hundreds of so-called Elvis performers strut their stuff with some good ones but also a lot of crap. I was getting anxious and couldn't wait to be called up. Finally, when it was my turn, I asked if it was necessary for me to change as I had brought along my white Elvis jumpsuit, and the director said OK, so off I went with my song, 'Until It's Time for Me to Go', and all of a sudden, I was blinded by a series of flashing and blinding camera lights of media reporters, and God knows who else. I felt like a mega star and couldn't believe what was happening as I carried on singing, unlike some of the other performers who were cut short by the director. When I finally finished, the director motioned me to come over to him.

I walked over quite nervously, and he said, 'That was great man. What's your name, and how come I haven't heard of you?' I said shyly, 'I've been around.' 'Are you in the musicians union? Or an Equity member?' to which I replied, 'I'm afraid not.' 'Then it's a closed shop for you, son, I'm afraid. I think you are the right man we're looking for. We need three Elvis, and you could play Elvis in his later years.'

Mr Cooney went on to say 'If I could get you an Equity members card, I'll try but can't promise. As far as I am concerned, I definitely would pick you. I need to kick off this show in two weeks, and I don't think it's possible to get you into Equity in two weeks as it's a closed shop, but I'll try. In the meantime, you go back and tell your local media that there is a possibility of you getting the part in the Elvis musical.' Whilst doing my audition, I later on discovered that one of the auditioners was the popular Shakin' Stevens, which later on I also discovered he was selected as the younger rockin' Elvis. I was ecstatic and went home with Joe on cloud nine. Yeah man!

When I contacted my local press, the *Croydon Advertiser*, a reporter came down and interviewed me, but as luck would have it, the paper went on a week's strike; therefore, a week later, the news was old hat. Plus, I didn't get the part as Elvis. Ray Cooney couldn't get me into Equity, and that was the end of my theatre deal. I don't know if this was divine intervention, but I got the feeling it was. As for some reason or the other, Jesus was protecting me from something that shouldn't happen, so I just accepted it as my destiny, although I cried and cried for a whole week or two. My wife, Zoe, was very supportive and gave me a lot of hope to be brave and carry on.

23 NORMAN AVENUE

I somehow managed to cope with the disappointment and carried on life as a normal family man. Then I decided for us to move to that place we'd seen about a year ago at 23 Norman Avenue as the owner decided to put it back on the market again. We made contact, and this time she put the price up. We thought that was a bit mean but carried on to negotiate. She finally settled for £24,000, £6,000 more than a year ago, but we wanted it badly, although I had to work extra hard now but according to my wife's tenacity and determination to move to a better location.

Thornton Heath was getting to be a real rough area compared with Sanderstead, with more room for three kids, Zoe and me. It was a four-bedroom semi with a lot more room and our very own garage and drive, beautiful gardens to the front and back. We moved in November 1978 and was one of the happiest families you could imagine, and from day 1, we started to redecorate and refurbish the whole place.

Our 4 bed semi and last family home
23 Norman Ave, Sanderstead, Surrey.

Duo – Graham and me

I formed a duo with a guy named Graham Edgerton. We did a lot of gigs and called ourselves Dewo. Graham and I got on very well, and one gig I remember we were playing for quite a posh do, and we turned up a bit late whilst the diners were already dining. When Graham and I were setting up, I accidentally did something and blew the fuse of the restaurant, and for a moment or two, the whole place was in darkness, and all I could hear Graham say, 'Trevor, what have you done?' The next thing I heard was one of the waiters crashing onto the floor in the dark. I don't know how we weren't slung out of there. I'll never know. Another time Graham and me were playing at a West End do in London at the pub called the Cockney Pride. Someone from the crowd approached me with a request written on a piece of paper, which I read as 'Sing happy birthday for Moo', which actually meant Mo, which is short for Maureen, and as I had read it as Moo, I sang, 'Happy birthday, dear Moo'. With that was a roar of laughter from the crowd, and Graham rolled up with laughter that he couldn't play his keyboard no more for a while. We had many a laughs, but we enjoyed it, all part of showbiz, I guess. Graham finally had to move up north to Leeds, and so we parted.

SPIDERWOOD FARM

This was my brother-in-law Joe's band consisting of Larry Smith on lead guitar, Steve Herbert on drums, Malcolm Watts on bass, Peter on keyboards and Joe (my bro-in-law) on rhythm guitar and vocals. I was their second vocalist; I did quite a few gigs with Spiderwood Farm, who later on changed the name to Stormpack. I sang all the Elvis, Chuck Berry, etc. We did a few Anglo Indian gigs and a few other gigs at posh hotels in London with a famous toastmaster called Ivor Spencer, and one of these gigs I remember was we had the Prime Minister, at that time was Harold Wilson, along with the MP Ted Heath. I was told to perform 'Teddy Bear' in front of Ted Heath, who roared with laughter, and Harold Wilson enjoyed it too with his famous pipe in his mouth. It went down brilliantly, and we got a few more posh gigs from Ivor Spencer.

When we were packing up our band gear and used the lift to load onto our van, there was a posh-looking gent in the same lift as us and happened to ask me a question. At the time, I used to smoke a pipe, and his question was 'What is the name of your band?' and me with my dodgy hearing replied, 'Clan', which was the name of the brand of tobacco I was smoking. At this reply of mine, the band boys rolled up in laughter. I looked puzzled, and the boys explained that the gent asked what the name of the band was and not my tobacco brand.

By the way, there were a few good moments when we were 'Stormpack', when we played at the Cricketers, South End; we played to a bunch of Hells Angels, all very mean-looking guys in leathers and tattoos all over. We were terrified as to how we'd go down with this lot. We eventually started nervously, and when we finished a couple of songs, there was silence, no applause whatsoever. I thought that we weren't going down too well, so I asked the band boys to take a break. 'Why did you stop?' one of the Hells Angels said. 'I thought we were not good enough,' I said. 'You guys are fuckin' brilliant. Please don't stop.' 'I thought you guys didn't approve as you didn't applaud.' 'Oh, that shit. We don't applaud. If we didn't think you were any good, you'd be out of here before you knew what was 'appening.' So we decided to carry on, and as I was doing my Elvis stuff, one of the Hells Angels' girlfriend came up to the stage and asked me for a kiss. The band boys all shook their heads for me not to even try it, so I moved away from her, and in doing so, the boyfriend of hers came up to me and said, 'You queer or something? Give her a kiss if she wants one', so I did, but she went the whole hog and snogged me proper. 'That's better,' said her boyfriend. The gig went down so well that in the end, they offered us another booking and said the next time we come, they would give us a motorbikes escort to the gig, and boy did they. When we arrived for the next gig, there were hundreds of motorbikes. We felt like royalty, and when we arrived at the Cricketers, there were posters everywhere, saying, 'Stormpack Are Back!'

Opportunity Knocks

In the year 1976, Elvis was still going strong with a constant threat from the Beatles, Rolling Stones, etc., but I was always a true Elvis fan and stayed loyal till today.

Whilst still working for the PO, there was a talent contest at PO headquarters. They had asked Hughie Green of the popular TV show *Opportunity Knocks* to compare the show. We got second place at this talent contest. Hughie then thought we were pretty good and suggested we audition for his TV show *Opportunity Knocks* with Spiderwood Farm. At the audition, which turned out to be a disaster, the band boys backing me got cold feet or were jealous that I as the lead singer would get all the attention from Hughie Green. With the result, we were a complete flop at the *Opportunity Knocks* audition, and all my dreams of stardom were shattered.

MANAGEMENT OFFERS

Ivor Spencer, the toaster master who had booked us boys to play at several posh functions, took a special interest in me apart from being a famous toastmaster he had meetings with MPs as well as HM the queen.

One fine day, Ivor asked me if he could be my manager. I was thrilled and honoured that Ivor should ask me this and immediately agreed, so Ivor started to draw up a contract and was interested in only me, which upset the rest of the band guys, but things didn't go so well with Ivor as he was always so busy with the Royals and MPs that he didn't have enough time to manage me properly. Finally, he came clean with me and said he didn't have enough time to devote to me as my manager and so ended what didn't even start. The rest of the band boys thought that I had deserved Ivor's refusal through pure jealousy. This had now caused a rift between the band and me. We started to drift apart.The last straw with Spiderwood was when I was leaving the band for a different management contract, with a new manager interested in me. That was the end of Spiderwood Farm/Stormpack.

CHAPTER 18

UNDER MANAGEMENT

My sister Maureen knew of this guy who was in showbiz/ entertainment business management. She arranged a meeting between him and me. This guy wanted to stay anonymous and to be referred to simply as my agent.

I made an appointment to meet my agent and found him very friendly, and so was his wife. They made us very welcome. I had taken Zoe along for this meeting, and we all gelled. Zoe explained that I was hard of hearing. He said he had a funny feeling I wasn't hearing him very well. I replied that I had impaired hearing and was quite ashamed of it. He replied that there was nothing to be ashamed of and that I had a gift to sing well, and that was all that mattered. He said he'd be interested in signing me up as my manager and promised to do his best to make me a big star.

He then started to work on me as he was quite influential and told me he had experience working with well-known celebs and had lots of experience to get me started on the road to stardom. He wanted to keep my Elvis style of singing but change it gradually to my own style. He started by making me outfits in a sort of Spanish-styled bolero costumes and still kept my Elvis white jumpsuit that I'd already had from the *Elvis* audition at the West End musical.

It was then in the meantime; I was offered a recording offer by a Gold merchant, who had a record label called Solid Gold, and the owner was promoting black artists with reggae music. My agent mentioned me to them about my record. They said that they would be interested in signing me on a contract to make records on their label. I was thrilled to bits and thought that this was the start of something big. We got to work immediately on a medley of Elvis hits.

This recording contract never happened as they had a disagreement with my agent.

Still employed at the PO, my agent thought up an idea to contact the BBC TV news and arranged an interview for the TV crew to interview me as this PO worker who sounded like Elvis, who has made a tribute record to his hero, Elvis. My agent said to the BBC that I was partly deaf and depended on vibrations to hear my music and that I'd give 20 percent as a donation to the society for the deaf. I was very nervous at this filming with the BBC crew. I was first filmed in an Elvis costume, which my agent had designed in a royal blue and silver lame trimmings and semi precious stones jumpsuit. The second part of this interview was in my PO uniform to express that I was still employed at the PO and would keep the job until I would make a hit and afford to give up the PO. I was asked about my hearing loss and was very nervous talking about it and felt ashamed and conscious about my hearing aid.

TT AT THE 'HARROW LEISURE CENTRE'

The year 1980, at Harrow Leisure Centre, was the first Anglo Indian reunion. My agent arranged for me to be star of the show. With my recent appearance on the BBC news at 6 p.m. and my recent record deal, I was king again. The gig went down very well, and I was now getting more and more famous within the Anglo Indian community.

It was now showtime again, and I was getting restless and itchy feet and longing to do my Elvis stuff again as I was getting on 46/47 years old, my agent organised with the Anglo Indian Association to do my stuff with a live band at the first Anglo Indian reunion dance held at Harrow, Middlesex. The dance was held at a huge aerodrome hanger, around 2,000 people from all parts of India, Calcutta, Bombay, Madras, Australia, USA and Canada.

The dance went on till 1 p.m. or 2 p.m., and of course, my band had a real fab evening with Roger Keys (the mad Irish, Jerry Lee Lewis on keyboards), Kenny Joseph on drums, Vince Wright on lead guitar and Tom on bass. The place was really rockin', and the crowd went wild with young females rushing on to the stage and wanting a piece of me in my royal blue Elvis jumpsuit. I got a bit carried away trying to reach out to the females that I stepped off the stage onto a table below the stage, and in doing so, the table collapsed with me sliding down the collapsing table. I managed to control my fall and made out, I wasn't hurt but later on discovered my right knee was swollen with pain after the gig. Roger the keyboard player was in fits of laughter, and so was the drummer Kenny, but all in all, it was a great gig, and we went home as kings of the road.

My agent was negotiating a deal for me to perform in my hometown, Bombay, at a branch of the Taj hotels called the President Hotel. The occasion was for New Year's Eve celebration on December 1981 to perform for an arranged fee for a week and flown out first class by Air India. I was in seventh heaven and couldn't sleep all night.

My Booking at Hotel President Bombay, 1981 'King Comes Home'

My agent and I left on 27 December 1981 for India, leaving Zoe very sad as she wanted to go to India as well, naturally as none of us had been back since 1960. After twenty-one years of going back sent shivers down my spine. the Indian newspapers had me in the headlines 'King Comes Home.' I was a superstar again.

I was so thrilled to be back after twenty-one years, and with tears in my eyes, I kissed the ground when we landed. I was greeted with style and chauffeur driven to our hotel for my stay at the President Hotel, a five-star hotel at Cuff Parade, Bombay. On my arrival, I was welcomed with a garland of flowers and escorted by security to my presidential suite on the seventeenth floor. I really felt like a king and was told by my agent to act like one. Immediately the very next day, I was interviewed by the Indian press and was given a warm welcome back. I really felt special and was now being swarmed by people who knew of my return home to Bombay from the UK. They were asking to see me but were being allowed only for a short period as I was not to be disturbed, and then there were the autograph hunters who all wanted a piece of me. I was escorted in the lifts and asked to wear my shades whilst being hurried to my awaiting chauffeur. Man I was ecstatic.

On 31 December 1981, I was to perform with the Gypsies Band of four lads flown in from Sri Lanka, who were very good musicians and backed me very well with just a couple of days practice and got my act ready in time for the New Year's show at the President's Hotel. A new stage was constructed for the band and me, and an extension to the stage was made especially for me so that I could walk or dance and do my thing reaching out to the audience. The stage floor was covered with red carpets, and it all looked super. I felt like a king.

When the thirty-first night finally arrived and the place was fully packed, the Gypsies band opened up with their stuff and played on for an hour to warm up the crowd, whilst I was getting ready and changed into my Elvis white jumpsuit, and then around 11 p.m., the band started the 2001 Space Odyssey intro to bring me on, and the houselights were dimmed, and after a huge drum roll, I strolled onto the stage, nervous at first, but the adrenaline was flowing and got me really pumped up.

There was a huge floodlight following me, which blinded me somewhat, that I could hardly see the audience. All I could see was all this sparkling amount of gold reflecting from the floodlights. At that moment, after I finished my first song of my repertoire, I quoted what I read about what John Lennon had said at one of his concerts: 'Those of you at the back there can applaud if you like, whilst those in the front can just rattle their jewellery'. It went down a treat, and from that moment on, there were rich Indian women whom I reached out to kiss their hands and were giving me wicked little sexy winks. My act went on for about an hour, after which I was drenched in sweat. I had done my full Elvis tribute act with a few Indian songs thrown in to keep the Indian crowd happy and returned for an encore. My opening show went off with a bang.

My agent was very excited with my performance and called for my wife, Zoe, to come and be with me for congrats after the show. All this time he had forbidden Zoe to be anywhere near me as I was supposed to be a single bachelor as he didn't like the idea of Zoe turning up in India as well, which she did on her own accord and arrived in Bombay with her mum. Like me, Zoe hadn't seen India for the last twenty-one odd years, No matter what the agent said, she was going to do what she wanted to do, so Zoe and I spent the night together.

Whilst my week's stay at the President I had to perform every night and during that week, there was the World Hockey Tournament held in Bombay, and my hotel was booked solid with all these international hockey champs from all over the world, including Argentina, Italy, Russia, India, Pakistan and scores of other countries. They attended my act every night, asking me for autographs. It was an honour. The booking for my week was over in a flash, so much so the management asked me to sign on for another week, which my agent and I agreed to gladly.

During this second week, I managed to go down memory lane with an old friend, Oscar, who was my guide to see the place where I lived at Dehdusty Building, Fort Street, Bombay, which I did, and to my amazement, my building where I stayed was 'demolished'. There I stood shocked and stunned with tears streaming down my face. I cried like a baby, thinking about all those years I grew up chasing kites, all those pimps and whores and all the wicked vices, all the fun we had growing up. I thought about my mum and dad; my sister Jean, who died at 16; my Teenage Rocker days, and I couldn't keep back the tears.

I went back to the President Hotel with Oscar and bid him farewell as I had to carry on with my second week's contract, which went off like a bomb as well and lots of write-ups in the local newspapers and, of course, autograph hunters wanting a piece of me.

Some were friends of old, and some I didn't know. Then it was all over and time to head back to England and my job at the post office, from riches to rags so to say, but I must say I was glad as two weeks with my agent was hell.

He had this temper on him, and I never knew when this volcano was going to erupt. I was glad it was all over, and Zoe and I were together at last, so we decided to have a week in Goa, India. We had the week of a lifetime, rode motorbikes, smoked dope, got drunk, swam in the nude and made friends with the ferryman, Bonny, who took us to his humble abode, a little shack by the beach, and his wife made us a meal of baby crabs curry and rice. After lunch, Bonny climbed the coconut tree for fresh coconuts for Zoe and me to eat and drink on a boat ride down the gentle river in the shade of the afternoon sun. We were in paradise. We returned to Bombay for our flight back to the UK.

Back in England, it was hard going back to the post office, with the Mickey taking. I had to brave it all and act as a normal postman again. My so-called contract with agent was more or less finished as he was a madman as far as Zoe and I were concerned. I would get nowhere with him and began to realise it was all over between the agent and me. Divine intervention!

CHAPTER 19

MY PO ACCIDENT

The year 1982 until 1987 were the last five years of my working life as a postman, until the day I had an accident whilst unloading the post office van. I trapped my right leg between the loading dock and the van, thereby causing me to lose my balance and fall. This fall twisted my knee ligaments. I was in agony and was rushed to hospital. I was treated with painkillers and thought no more of it, until a few days later, my knee swelled up. I saw my GP, who laid me off work for two weeks, which turned to months off work with this painful and swollen knee.

I was now more off work sick than actually attending work. I tried claiming damages from the PO for my accident at work. With the greatest of difficulty, the PO union managed a paltry of £350, which then was quite a lot of money to me, so like a fool, I accepted it as I didn't want any more hassle as this went on and on for years, trying to get a better payoff from the PO. I could have if I fought a little harder, but by the end of 1987, I had really had it with the PO and would do anything to get out.

I was given lighter duties at the PO in the office doing clerical work. I hated it. It was a 9-to-5 job, and it was getting me down, until I was called in for an operation on my right knee to correct my damaged ligaments. After this operation, my right knee was never the same, and until today I still suffer with a slight limp and causes pains in my back. I could have had thousands in compensation from the PO but gave up without a fight. I must have been the biggest idiot in those days. All I wanted was to finish with the PO, which finally happened in the year 1989.

After a few years being off sick, the PO decided to retire me at the age of 48 on medical grounds. I was ecstatic. This was what I wanted and didn't care what they would offer me in compensation. I just wanted out and finally was retired early on medical grounds from the PO for a paltry sum of £9,000 and an early weekly pension, which at the time I thought was a lot of money compared with the thousands I could have fought for. That was me now, a faded and failed Trevor Elvis and now a retired early postie.

The operation took its toll. I had to learn to literally walk again and spent a few years at our home in Norman Avenue. Being on the sick, I managed to still do a lot of work and changes to our house, and as my leg got better, I started to get the urge to form a band of musicians and started to get a few gigs at the local pubs and social clubs with a few Anglo boys, which I was never ever happy with as they never backed me the way I wanted to be backed. I tried to hold practices at my house, but they weren't really interested. Plus, playing at some of the boring English social clubs was soul-destroying as I'd give it all with my singing, and the crowds didn't give a monkey's, even if you were Elvis Presley himself. All they were interested was their silly old cursed Bingo and didn't give a shit who was performing. I eventually got sick of it and gave up the idea of my own band for a while until I got the urge again later on.

Until I met Ian Gomes, an excellent pianist who played regular at a pub at Peckham and was looking for a singer, so I went along with an Anglo friend, Albert Ennis (who passed away a few years now). Albert, who sang and sounded like Frank Sinatra, introduced me to Ian Gomes. Ian and I hit it off immediately in the Golden Lion at Peckham and then later on at the Albion pub at South Norwood every Thursday night. This went on for a year or two until Ian moved on to bigger venues such as the Ritz and Savoy of posh London hotels playing classical piano and jazz standards.On one of Zoe's birthdays,

I asked Ian Gomes since he was playing at the Ritz in London if it was possible to book us a table for high tea at the Ritz. As it was quite expensive, I decided to give Zoe a treat, especially with Ian playing there as well. Ian asked me later on to hang on as Frank Sinatra was coming over, but I'd already booked a cab on the round trip. Zoe was ecstatic and had a wonderful birthday surprise, although we missed the chance to meet old Blue Eyes.

I started to get itchy and wanted to try again to form a better bunch of guys to back me, so I put an ad in the local rag and got a reply from a guitarist from Manchester Vince Wright, a tall English lad with a northern accent. He was a good guitarist and was keen to practice and form a proper band. I put another ad in for a pianist in the Jerry Lee Lewis style and almost immediately got a response from an Irish mad man Roger Keys, who was daft as a brush but very good on the ivories. He had an old, beat-up keyboard and promised to get a better one soon, but it never happened as Roger was a compulsive gambler and was also a good chippie, who laid wooden floors and was paid fairly well. Roger, Vince and I teamed up with a bass player called Tom, who had a good job as a manager with some big company and lived in quite a fancy house somewhere in Crawley. Tom had spare keyboards, guitars, amplifiers, PA systems the lot, so we used to practice at Tom's. Then of course, Roger was loaned a keyboard from Tom, who said he never ever heard his keyboards sound as it did till only after he heard them played by Roger.

Roger had an offer to appear on Sky TV on a show called *Starsearch* and wanted us to come along as his backing band, which we decided to go along to the London studios. It turned out to be a sort of competition TV show called *Starsearch*. Before we went along, we had a rough rehearsal with Vince, Roger, a drummer Ken Joseph (passed away sadly last year, 2013) and me. Tom the bass player couldn't make it, so Roger hired a session bass player from somewhere in North London, where Roger lived in Camden Town. The TV show went off with a bang as it was a competition to search for a star. We were now in it, and if we'd won that series, we would have to come again to compete for another series, but to our good or bad luck, we came second and didn't qualify for the next round. Divine intervention again?

CYPRUS

In between waiting for my knee op, my beautiful darling wife, Zoe, kept on working hard as ever at Phillips with computers as a programmer analyst and was doing really well. She decided to book a holiday to Cyprus, and boy what a holiday that turned out to be. Zoe, our youngest daughter Nicky, Zoe's mum, her brother Joe and girlfriend Mary and me all stayed at Limasol, Cyprus, for two weeks, until the day I happened to sing with the Cypriot band that was playing one of the evenings. My bro-in-law Joe offered to play guitar with the band to accompany me whilst I sang a couple of Elvis stuff.

Then all hell broke loose. The management went wild with excitement with my performance and wanted me to do it again for his wife and family to hear me. I agreed to fix another date, and the boss was very pleased, so I went off to enjoy the rest of my holiday. Zoe and I decided to hire a Mini Moke to explore the island, so off we went in our open-air mini bombing down the open roads of Cyprus and went up mountain roads and seen all the sights until we heard a spluttering sound from the engine and discovered we were running out of gas. We couldn't tell how much gas was in the tank as the petrol gauge was not working. We then discovered we were out of gas. We had now broken down and waited to flag down a passing motorist for help with no luck.

Until this lorry driver being a local stopped suddenly for us and couldn't speak much English. We managed to tell him we were out of gas. He seemed to understand immediately and offered to drive us to the nearest gas station to buy a gallon, which the lorry guy filled in his container, and then drove us back to our mini. We were so grateful and offered the guy some money, but he wouldn't take it, so he went off, and whilst doing so, his lorry, which was parked on a verge off the road, was now having difficulty getting out of a ditch. Zoe and I tried to help by giving him a hand at trying to push this heavy lorry with no luck. The guy told us not to worry and that he'd sort himself out as he was a local and would get some help sooner or later.

We thanked him again and drove off back to our hotel. By now, we were really late for my arranged time to perform for the manager at the King Alfred Hotel with his wife and family. Then what an evening it turned out to be. We apologised for arriving late as we explained our misadventure with the mini. The manager was very glad we arrived and looked forward to seeing us at the bash, with full dinner and drinks laid on free for Zoe, her family and me. We all got VIP treatment. My performance went off like a bomb, and the manager and his family were all very excited and thanked me very much, with more drinks on the house for us all. By now, I was pretty pissed, and the band started playing their Cypriot music, and then the local people, mainly guys, started local stuff and dancing round in a circle and kicking their legs higher and higher with the exciting music, until I decided to join them, and then all hell broke loose.

I got a bit carried away, trying to keep up with them, and lifted my legs a little bit more than I could, and then bang, I was on the floor and discovered my dodgy right knee couldn't cope with the excessive strain and swelled up like a balloon. I was in excruciating pain, and of course, the management was really worried about me. Their 'star' performer was now injured. I was carried off by the rest of the locals, and there was this guy whilst I was on the floor, rolling with pain. He had a camera and was taking pics of me in pain and thought it was one of my funny act I was putting on. I felt like ramming his camera up his arse and swore at him. 'You think that's funny MF?'

I was eventually rushed to the local hospital and spent the rest of our holiday with my leg bandaged up and in crutches. The manager was very apologetic, gave me and the family extra care and offered us an extra room for our luggages and extra stay before our flights back home. The manager then offered me a contract to return to Cyprus as an entertainer, and I said that I'd go back and let him know, but it never happened.

MY MEDICAL RETIREMENT

The day finally arrived to see the regional medical officer to check out my injured right knee to see if I was able to go back to work in the PO for active duties. I arrived nervously with my hearing aid 'on'. Before entering the building in my nervous state, I turned my hearing aid 'off' as I found the noise of the passing traffic was too loud and was bothering me.

I entered the building and greeted the receptionist and showed her my appointment letter. She asked me to take a seat and wait until I was called. I must have been called a few times, but I never heard my name being called, until a nurse finally came and tapped me on the shoulder and said, 'Mr Taylor?' I nodded yes nervously, and then she motioned me to a cubicle to get changed into my shorts and take my shoes off for the examination. I was waiting for quite some time to be called, and then after about twenty minutes or so, the cubicle door was flung open by a very angry and red-faced medical officer, who said in a very loud and irritated voice, 'Mr Taylor, I've been calling out to you for the last ten to twenty minutes! PLEASE step out so I can examine you!'

I did step out and was wondering why this doctor was so het up. He then asked me to 'tiptoe', which I understood it meant to touch my toes, so I did. The doc's face was now getting redder and said, 'No, when I say tiptoe, I mean like.' He demonstrated to me by lifting his heels and standing on the tips of his toes. I replied, 'Oh I see.' He just nodded quite grumpily with a half smile.

He then motioned me to get on the couch to examine my dodgy right knee and kept bending it at various angles to check it out for pains and movements, and each time he asked me a question, I kept replying 'pardon' several times as I couldn't hear him clearly. I could see he was getting more and more agitated, and in the end, he motioned for me in a loud and angry, frustrated red face and said, 'Get dressed now!' quite abruptly. I went to get dressed and waited to be called again.

After quite a while, the nurse came to tell me the doc was ready to see me again, so I did as told. As I approached the doc's desk, he just motioned to me without saying a word and pointing to the door outside the building, I wondered what he meant and asked the nurse what the doc meant. She just nodded and said with a half smile, 'Yes, you are free to go home now.' I said, 'Now? Is it over?' She nodded again with a half-forced smile. 'Yes, yes', her face looking flushed and trying to look pleased with me. I wondered why.

Until I left the building and wondered why the traffic was so quiet, I had forgotten to turn my hearing aid 'BACK ON'. Wow, I wondered now what a confusion I caused with the RMO.

I waited to see my GP, Dr Sudhi, to get the results of the RMO examiner. My GP said to me, 'Well, Trevor, it looks good news for you', and I asked why. And he replied, 'The RMO you saw a couple of weeks ago does NOT want to see you again EVER.'

Dr Sudhi then said, 'It looks good for you, Trevor, as he's passed you medically unfit for LIFE and does not EVER want to see you again.' 'Oh' was all I could say. I was in a state of shock.

Then Dr Sudhi asked me since I was not working now if I would consider being his chauffer for a year as he was on a drink driving ban, not that it was his fault. He explained that he'd only had a couple of glasses of wine for lunch and was unlucky to be stopped by a rookie cop who didn't quite know him as all the other cops knew Dr Sudhi well as he attended and worked with the cops with criminal cases. I agreed to take on the job as chauffer for Dr Sudhi at £5 per hour, which he agreed.

I am now a chauffeur for my doctor at £5 per hour and feeling mighty proud of it. I'll be driving him for a whole year, man! What a packet I will earn!

Whilst parking the car and waiting for the doc on his visit to one of his patients, I fell asleep as I was tired of reading my newspaper. After over an hour or so, I was awoken by the doc, who knocked on the glass window of my door. I awoke quite suddenly, only to be awoken to the smell of strong booze. I said to the doc that he smelt like a brewery, and he replied, 'Oh, I always have a quick one with this patient.' 'Quick one,' I replied. 'I better not light a fag, Doc. I might blow us both up.'

It was getting close to Christmas, and one of the days, as I dropped the doc home, he asked me to wait a minute and popped into his house and returned with a bottle of whisky. He wished me a happy Christmas. I thanked him and asked him if he'd like to join me later to share the drink with me. He said, Not today as I have my practice party.' And I innocently replied to the doc, 'Practice party, when is the REAL one?' The doc thought I was telling him one of my jokes, and being funny, he replied, 'Oh, Trevor . . .'

I got indoors and told Zoe what the doc had just said about the practice party and that I replied and asked the doc when was the real party, and Zoe said to me, 'You didn't, did you?' and me being completely unaware that the 'practice' was referred to as the doctor's surgery, I dropped a terrible clanger. I was so naive. I suppose coming from India and not used to these terms and expressions, I was sometimes innocently unaware of expressions such as when I first was admitted to Mayday Hospital in Croydon and was asked by the nurse on her examination questions, 'Have you spent a penny?' I replied, 'No, I don't have any money,' and the nurse replied quite exasperatedly, 'Have you been wee-wee?' I replied, 'Oh, oh no, not yet.' Funny country, this I thought. Why can't they speak simple English?

I was now a part-time driver/chauffer for my doc and waiting now to be officially medically retired from the post office, and then I was finally interviewed at home by one of the PO officials and was told I was being offered early medical retirement. Because of my past medical attendance, the PO was making me an offer of £9,000, which I thought at the time was wonderful and didn't realise that a few years later, I could have had thousands more in compensation from the PO because of my accident being on the work's premises, but I had had enough of twenty years' service and wanted out. Especially that Maggie Thatcher was the Prime Minister in charge, and things were getting tougher at the PO.

On my official retirement day at the PO, Mr Pond, the postmaster of my office, was there in my farewell party arranged by the PO union leader, Mr Dai Reece, and the postmaster, Mr Pond, who also knew me as Elvis, asked why was I leaving, and I told him it was on medical grounds. He just laughed it off and thought I was joking.

One of the days I was at home on medical retirement, I engaged myself with a lot of household chores, and one of them was to build a fishpond at my rear garden, which I did very well to my surprise. Then I turned my hand at gardening and thought I'd surprise Zoe with planting and growing some chillies. She always said growing your own chillies was bad luck, so I decided to prove her wrong and proceeded to rake the soil and planted the chilli seeds.

After a while of planting the chilli seeds, I started to feel a burning sensation on my penis, and as time went on, it got worse. I then felt I wanted to wee and suddenly felt a terrible burning sensation as I was making wee. Only then did I realise that I'd forgotten to wash my hands before I decided on a wee. The burning got worse until Zoe arrived back from work, I told her that I was in terrible pain and told her about the chillies. She laughed at first but then decided to help me. She told me to strip off and lie on the bed spread-eagled on my back and hurried along, got a bowl of ice and started to place the ice cubes on my burning penis, and being spread-eagled, she started to cool me down with a fan. It started to give me some relief. Sex was out of the question for months!

CHAPTER 20

U S OF AMERICA, THE LAND OF MY DREAMS! (THE LAND OF ELVIS)

Our Hawaiin tour of Honolulu, Kuwaii and Maui. 1986.

This £9,000 from the PO for my compensation was a blessing in disguise that I wanted to celebrate by going on a really good holiday. Zoe and I were friendly with an English builder who was self-employed, and since I was now retired, this builder (George) employed me as a skivvy, basically a tea boy, and paid me for the help. George and his wife, Rita, were friendly with my wife, Zoe, and me. George and Rita got friends with us, and we started socialising a bit until we mentioned to them that we were interested on going on a holiday tour of the States, the USA, that is, as it had always been my dream to see the USA, so we started preparing for it. That was when George suggested that he and Rita would like to join us. We thought about it for a while and then agreed we'd go for it after we planned our own itinerary from the East to West Coast of America, including Hawaii. Wow, I never even dreamt that we could do it, and after an intensive preparation by my clever wife, Zoe, we planned to tour the States, the four of us.

It was the year 1986 that we did the extensive tour starting with the Big Apple. When we landed at John F Kennedy Airport, we finally got out of security and proceeded to our first stay at Motel 6, as we were advised to book with them throughout our stay in the US. WOW, were we impressed with New York and all its hustle and bustle and magnificent skyscrapers and, of course, the Empire States building and Grand Central Station, and listening to all those Yanks speaking in their American accent was unbelievable. I've seen a lot of American movies but never ever heard an American speaking live. It was funny to hear them speaking like that as if it wasn't real. I thought they only spoke that way in the movies.

We planned to stay in the United States for about five weeks and had planned to stretch our money very carefully; it was also a great feeling spending US dollars for the first time of our lives. We managed quite well in New York until we went to the Hyatt, one of the expensive hotels, for a drink and nearly choked on it when the bill arrived. We also were planning on booking a trip to Hawaii, if we got a good deal, so off we went to this travel agent, and she happened to be very helpful. A fat middle-aged Yank with her cool American accent managed to sort out a real good deal for us in Hawaii. All the while she had a fag in her mouth, and whilst sorting out different options, she kept saying on the phone to us, 'Not baad', in her Yank accent, and I kept repeating after her in my American imitation, 'Not baaad', and the poor elderly lady wasn't a bit the wiser if I was serious or not.

My 'wonder woman' wife, Zoe, had planned our whole itinerary and planned our next move to San Francisco. Wow, she worked out internal flights, seventeen in all within the States, St Louis being the hub, and connected to different parts of the States we planned to visit. San Francisco was real cool, man. We stayed there a few nights. We drove down the 'crockedest street in the world' and had some crazy fun, Frisco the hippy city and the Golden Gate bridge. Oh yes, George hired a cool American chevvie and did all the driving, and I did all the videos, saw Alcatraz and all that jazz.

Next stop was Colorado, a bit more cooler than Frisco and LA. We started to enjoy a bit of the old Western town and a bit of the red-necked Yanks and noticed a different yank accent there. We stayed there a couple of nights and moved on to our next plan, Florida. George hired another cool chevvi, and we drove along the Florida Keys, which seemed to never end, and of course, it was in the month of September and baking hot compared with cool Colorado. we enjoyed our stay and were getting used to living out of our suitcases. Until on to our next move, New Orleans, man, it was something else. It brought back memories of the movie *King Creole* and Elvis singing 'Dixieland Rock', and all the rest sent shivers down my spine. The French quarter of Orleans with all those buildings with those fancy balconies and railings, just like the movie with Elvis singing 'Crawfish', we stayed at an old bawdy-looking hotel maybe for hookers or something like that. The landlady with a fag in her mouth and a real fat mama and the red decor gave the impression of a whorehouse, but we stayed on and enjoyed 'Bourbon Street', a wicked old street with its jazz joints and seedy shows. We managed to have 'Gumbo', a sticky New Orleans special; I was the only one who enjoyed it. We enjoyed all the Dixieland Jazz and numerous buskers and then took a trip on the New Orleans Steam boat, including dinner and a jazz band on board and a sunset cruise. Man it was crazy fun, what with me being told off for doing a video of the jazz band, which was forbidden. We enjoyed it all the same until our next move, Nashville, Memphis, Tennessee, wow, wow, wow.

Welcome to Nashville, Tennessee, home of country music USA. Man, I really loved country music. It was part of Elvis's music, and I sure did dig it. We saw a few country artists performing in their original country styles and went on a tour seeing homes of the famous stars such as Dolly Parton, Conway Twitty and, of course, the famous Gran Ol' Opry, which sadly was closed in the month of September. One of the things that impressed me was the Tennessee cops. We were sitting in a Tennessee cafe when two Tennessee cops arrived into the diner with their cool dark blue outfits. I had my video on them and trying to do it secretly until one of the cops happened to notice what I was doing and said to me, 'Is that a movie thaang there, man?' and me being caught out nervously replied, 'Yes, yes, Officer', but these cool cops didn't seem to mind and wanted me to carry on with the video and took their guns out of their holsters and twirling the guns around their fingers and really showing off, and then I took advantage to video their cop cars, and they were really cool about it. I noticed the difference of the friendliness of the deep South compared with the cold and brash New Yorkers. I was also impressed with the New York yellow cabs though, reminded me of Marylyn Monroe and the movie *The Seven-Year Itch* and of course not forgetting the Frisco, black-and-white cop cars and the Frisco cops in their cool uniforms like in *The Streets of San Francisco*' and Tony Benet and all that jazz.

Las Vegas was also visited when we booked a Greyhound bus at night and arrived in Vegas at 6 a.m., all sleepy and blurry-eyed at the Stardust motel. Before checking in, we walked into the casino, and it seemed like it was never shut, all lit up as daylight, slot machines and roulette tables all in full swing. I had to rub my eyes to realise I wasn't dreaming, so out came my video camera, and I started shooting, only to be tapped on the shoulder. 'Sorry, sir, no videos in here.' Damn it, again!

We went to see Fats Domino performing live at the International Hotel, where Elvis performed, only to find a life-size plaque in the foyer to remember his performances there. Fats was brilliant and mentioned Elvis singing one of his hits, 'Blueberry Hill'. I was in tears.

GRACELAND, HOME OF THE KING

At last, Elvis's home, what can I say? Was I sad? Was I happy, or what?

After all those years of waiting to catch a glimpse of my hero, Elvis, or even get close to seeing him in person, only to live with his memories of my dead hero, was what I had to be content with, so I braved on with much sadness to go on the tour of Graceland, only to be told 'no videos or flash photos'. I was so put off as I had my video camera ready to shoot. I was about to abort the tour but was encouraged by Zoe to carry on. I did so very reluctantly and was more than impressed with what I saw. His decor was exactly what I'd imagined, very garish but suited his image; I loved his 'jungle room' and the collection of his stage outfits, his hall with his golden and platinum awards and the achievements in the short space of time that he lived. The amount of movies and songs he recorded was unbelievable. He was my true hero and will be till the day I die. Elvis memories will live forever. God bless his soul.

When we came out of the tour of Graceland, we were taken to see the *Lisa Marie* aeroplane, Elvis's private jet, named after his daughter, fitted with gold taps and posh leather suits, phones, TV, etc. Wow!

The tour was finished and no video to prove it. I was quite disappointed with the tour and quite upset because I wasn't allowed to take any videos of my lifetime hero's house, so we wandered about a bit outside Graceland and were outside a place called Heartbreak Hotel. I was impressed with a huge Cadillac Convertible in a beautiful light blue and white leather seats. I immediately got out my video camera and was suddenly interrupted by an American voice, 'Do you like muh car?' I turned round to see this red-faced, tall, friendly Yank, and I replied, 'I sure do, man. Man, that's one hell of a car.' 'Well, do you want a ride in it?' said he. 'Well, we'd be very much obliged, my wife and me and my friend George and his wife, if you won't mind?' 'Sure as hell,' said the man, who introduced himself as Noel. 'Hop in, you guys, and I'll take you on a tour round Memphis. I was born and raised in Memphis, and you guys come from England to see Elvis's home and that you see, I grew up with Elvis and played soccer with him long ago.' Noel asked me if my video camera had sound on it because I was giving a recorded commentary as I was being driven, and I said, 'Sure, Noel, my camera records sound as well.' 'That's what I figured,' said Noel.

So we drove along Memphis, and Noel suggested I would get better shots of Memphis and retracted the sun roof so that I could stand up on his front passenger seat and get better views of Beale Street as we passed a huge bunch of kids also touring and shouted out at me and my camera, 'Hi, mum!' We passed a huge bronze statue of Elvis in Beale Street and was told it was the only statue of a white man in that area as it was a strictly black area where Elvis grew up and shopped in Beale Street for his flashy clothes in pimp shops. Noel finally dropped us off near a bus stop as we wanted to get back we exchanged addresses with good old Noel and headed back to our motel.

The next day, we went down the famous Beale Street, which was cordoned off from the traffic at night, and there were buskers, one better than the other. We were spoilt for choice, mostly black musicians belting out their stuff, mostly blues and R & B stuff. You couldn't sit still. Guys were dancing and doing all kinds of stuff. Cops on horseback to keep order. There were a few shops open where Elvis used to shop for his first guitar and those pimp clothes.

We now had our minds set on visiting Hawaii, *Blue Hawaii*, another one of Elvis's movies. We arrived from LA on a flight to Honolulu, and man were we impressed. The local Hawaiian people were so friendly. 'Aloha' meant hello, goodbye and everything. A day or so in Honolulu and we moved on to Maui, another one of the Hawaiian islands, where we had a magnificent lau festival on the beach with so much beauty and colour of everyone dressed in beautiful-coloured Hawaiian shirts, skirts and the beauty of the setting sun. We had this most amazing evening of Hawaiian music with exotic dancers and a sumptuous meal of specially roasted pig and plenty of Mai Tais and Blue Hawaii's to drink.

Whilst in Honolulu, we met a friend who was married to an American in the US forces. Her name was Caroline. She passed away now. Bless her soul. She took us to this PX shop, especially for the guys from the forces, where they sold heaps of Hawaiian shirts, skirts, dresses, and guess what, I ended up with a dozen or so shirts as they were a real bargain at forces prices I couldn't refuse.

From Maui, we moved on to Kuwaiti, another exotic island, and stayed there for two days. I hired my own car this time and toured the island, just Zoe and me, as I was pretty fed up not driving myself and being driven by George all the time. We've now at the end of our US tour and ready sadly to head home to England, but it sure was an exciting experience we'll never forget. That was the year 1986. I'll never forget.

CHAPTER 21

KENYA SAFARI, MAURITIUS AND SEYCHELLES

In 1987, the following year, Zoe's mum decided to treat us and her other two daughters, Olga and Audrey, and their husbands, Eddie and Ted, and her son Joe and his wife, Mary, on a holiday to Kenya and a Safari trip, including Mauritius and Seychelles, which started with Kenya and the Safari trip to stay at the famous Tree Tops to watch the wild animals.

We had an experience when a wild panther came up the hillside whilst we were at breakfast. I never saw people move away so fast, including myself, as this black panther calmly came up this hill to find something to eat for its young ones. The waiters were used to it coming now and then fed it with scraps of food and leftovers. I was with my video camera ready to film the panther, but when everyone started to run for their lives, so did I. I ran to the nearest toilet and locked myself in until I heard the all clear.

We were woken up early the next day for an early morning Safari in separate jeeps and saw loads of wild animals and had a great day. We stayed by the Zamburu River and saw loads of crocodiles and wildlife until we moved on to Mauritius and stayed at the famous La Pirogue, where we had our own little cottages on this beautifully maintained complex. All meals were included in the evening. We had wonderful entertainment and were entertained by very good Mauritian musicians.

Then Trevor Elvis had to strike again and make his mark. I plucked up enough courage to chat up one of the musicians during their break and asked them if I could do a few songs with them. They didn't seem to mind at all, and then I took to the stage eventually. All hell broke loose. I got a thunder of applause and was asked to do an encore and another encore. I finally thanked the band, and everyone was really pleased. I was the star of Mauritius, and I did not know. That after a few years later, there were photos of me at the La Pirogue as mentioned to me by one of my friends John DeCosta, who is a Mauritian, and went back home to visit his parents in Mauritius. 'You are a really famous star in Mauritius at the La Pirogue. I saw your photos in the showcase.'

From Mauritius, we moved on to Seychelles. Man it was paradise, so beautiful I wouldn't know where to start, the most beautiful beaches, birds and sand and sea. We had three to four days there I'll never forget.

OUR TWENTY-FIFTH WEDDING ANNIVERSARY

When we married in 16 December 1961, we could not afford a big wedding celebration as I was 21, and Zoe was 16/17, so we did not have a big reception or anything of the sort, so in the year 1986, twenty-five years later, we could finally afford to have a big bash, so Zoe and I decided to do it in style. We had a special Mass at St Gertrude's Catholic Church with Fr John Watts, renewing our marriage vows, and then followed it by a big reception at the church hall with a live band, exotic foods and plenty of booze. We had about two hundred guests, and it all went down a treat, never to be forgotten. It was worth waiting the twenty-five years, and we thank the Lord for his blessings even till today.After this fabulous wedding ceremony, Wonder Woman Zoe and I were planning a fabulous sea cruise, which was to be a second honeymoon, so we made the plan.

Our Wedding Anniversary!

Sea Cruise arranged by my Wonder Woman.

Our very dear German friends left to right Maggie and Bob
(from Baden Baden); Rita, George and Zoe and I behind.

CHAPTER 22

THE MS SEAWARD SEA CRUISE

B ack to England and the year is 1988/89, I was now officially retired from the post office and wanted to celebrate my retirement. Zoe and I were now getting interested and keen on a sea cruise as I'd never experienced a luxurious liner because the boat I came into England was only a cheap cargo boat. My friend George and his wife, Rita, also got interested and wanted to come along, especially after our very enjoyable US tour, so we planned this sea cruise. It was my very first trip on this luxury liner, and boy what a cruise that was, right up my street. It was a 1950s theme cruise, with rock 'n' roll every day for two weeks. We embarked at Southampton, where the ship was docked, for our trip to Orlando, and before sailing off, we had these posh welcome drinks and then shown our cabins with our own TV, shower, wardrobes and room service at the call from your room phone. The TV had continuous rock 'n' roll all day long – Elvis, Jerry Lee, Fats Domino, Chuck Berry, the lot. Man I was in my glory. All we did was eat, eat and booze from a.m. to p.m., with entertainment from morning till night on deck and at the pool. In the evening were dancing and cabaret shows of famous stars which we were lucky to have such as the Platters and the Four Aces. Talking about the Platters in particular,I must tell you how I met 'Herbie' from the Platters.

I woke up one morning on the cruise and decided to have before breakfast the 'eye-opener' as it was called. It was fresh coffee, doughnuts, etc., and whilst waiting in the queue, I was behind this black guy who had no shirt on. I couldn't help noticing his massive gold chain, gold rings and bracelets, so I said, 'Man, that's some fancy gold you have there.' 'Oh, thanks,' said he. 'My name is Herbie, from the Platters.' I nearly fell through the floor. 'The one and only Platters, man, you were my favourite guys. You know, Herbie, when I was in India, Bombay, in 1957, we had no TV, and the only way we heard of you guys was on the radio or the jukeboxes or the movies. I'll never forget the day I saw you guys. It was in the movie *The Girl Can't Help It*, and you were the guy that sang bass in a song called "You'll Never Know".' Herbie then replied with a rapturous laugh and said, 'Hey, man, how about that, would you like to come to my table over there and meet the rest of the Platters and tell them what you just told me? You see, these guys and one girl are all new members to the Platters and would be really interested to hear your story.' I was elated. Here I was, sitting and chatting to these world-famous stars. I was in heaven.

Herbie as it turned out asked me if I was a fan of Elvis. 'Why did you ask me that?' I answered. He said, 'I noticed an Elvis buckle on your belt.' And I said, 'Sure as hell I am.' He then told me that he and Elvis met at a casino in Las Vegas, and Elvis presented him with the gold bracelet he had on his wrist. I asked him how Elvis was, and he told me that Elvis was a real generous guy and very humble and friendly. He looked even more handsome in person than all those movies and photos. Herbie then invited me that same evening to sit on the front row during his performance so that he could sing personally to me and my wife. Man, I was blown away.

We made a few stops on this cruise – Jamaica, Cayman Islands, Mexico – all very short day trips but lovely to see such exotic places, would have loved to see at a better and longer space of time.

Whilst on this cruise, we met a German couple, Rupert Killian and his wife, Maggie. Whilst having dinner the first night on the MS *Seaward* ship, Maggie seemed very friendly and was smartly dressed, and so was Bob, her hubby, who never spoke a word of English compared with Maggie, who spoke good English in her German accent. She wanted some help from Zoe with the menu and translated some of the menu items, and Zoe obliged immediately. Bob just kept smiling; we helped them out. After dinner, Zoe and I wanted to have a smoke, and as we were on a no smoking table, we asked Maggie to pardon us as we wanted to move to a smoking table. Maggie was shocked that she was going to lose us and said, 'Oh no, we don't mind you sitting here and smoking. Please do not move away. Bob and I would love you to stay', so we did and got chatting together with our friends George and Rita. Maggie got to like Zoe very much, and when we exchanged addresses, Maggie said she and Bob would love us to visit them in Germany any time we wished.

GERMANY, BADEN BADEN

On visiting Germany for the very first time, we didn't have a clue regarding Bob and Maggie's lifestyle and only later on discovered that Maggie and Bob were really wealthy. On our first visit to their home in Baden Baden, Germany, by train, we asked a German guy if we were on the right train to Baden Baden as he said yes, and with a friendly smile, he then added that Baden Baden was a beautiful place and noted for its spas and natural springs, and by the way, only the rich and famous live there. Wow, we didn't have a clue, so we carried on. When we arrived at the station, we phoned our new friend Maggie, and she told us to wait a while as her hubby, Bob, and she was coming to pick us up quite soon, 'yah, yah, nix, nix and all that'. The jolly couple met us with warm German hugs and welcome. Maggie and Bob were about ten to fifteen years older than us; we got on like a house on fire. Maggie loved to sing and sang all those Second World War songs of Lily Marline, and Bob flourished me with German beer and all sorts stocked in his bar. They had a cellar room downstairs. They called it their hobby room, where Maggie had an electric keyboard; we had a lot of singing, dancing and drinking and a load of fun and laughter. Maggie turned out to be a real live wire, and Bob was this distinguished silver-haired German gentleman who never spoke much English but got on with a few words from a little help from us and Maggie. Bob and I had good conversations. Although I didn't know German nor did he English, we got on very well, especially after a few drinks my German started to get better.

Bob and Maggie suggested they take us to their German social club for drinks and entertainment and Bob and Maggie having heard I was an entertainer in the UK. After a few drinks, Bob got hold of a guitar and urged me to sing and entertain them, and of course, I was quite tipsy by then and got up enough courage with this German crowd. I thought to, *Oh yes, didn't Elvis do 'Wooden Heart' in German?* so I thought, why not? Let them have it in the German version I knew. So I got up and sang aloud, 'Muse den muse den . . .' and the rest of it.

Bob was a wonderful, warm and friendly German gentleman, and so was Maggie, his second wife. Maggie had three sons from her previous marriage, and Bob had two daughters from his previous marriage and was a very wealthy man with his own fire extinguishing business and owned a hotel at Oberammergau near the Austrian border. Bob treated Zoe and me very well during our stay and took us to all the top restaurants, especially when he drove us to France for the day to treat us with frog legs, a French speciality, and whilst in Baden Baden itself, we were treated to the famous thermal spas for the day, with special saunas, steam rooms, etc.

Then in Germany, it was very different from the UK or what I never experienced before, when Bob suggested we go for a sauna, just him and me. Maggie and Zoe were not interested, so Bob and I carried on, and Bob led the way to the changing lockers. He told me that I should put away my swimming trunks into the locker and head for the sauna completely in the nude. Man, this was crazy. How was I supposed to now walk completely nude all the way to the sauna?

I was now feeling quite embarrassed to walk nude, but then suddenly, I had to stop myself from laughing as a rather fat bloke with a big rounded belly walked about quite calmly in the nude, and what was funnier was that he had only a little penis you could just about notice it. Then even funnier still was the next thing I noticed a skinny tall man was walking by, and he had a mighty big whopper on him. I had to control myself from becoming hysterical but carried on towards the sauna with Bob. When we reached the sauna, I noticed everyone was in the nude, so I did not try to hide my little winkle anymore and went to sit on the bench, only to discover it was red-hot, so I kinda jumped slowly, trying not to show the pain. There was a young girl in there as well, and she sort of gave a slight giggle watching me. Sitting there, I suddenly discovered my wristwatch had a metal strap and was getting hotter by the minutes and started to take it off slowly and held it in my hands for a bit, with more giggles from this nude girl again, until I had had enough and decided to quit. Bob followed me, and we carried on to meet Zoe and Maggie.

Now Zoe hadn't experienced the sauna and also wanted to try it. I told her all about the nude stuff, and she said she wouldn't mind, just as long it was going to be just her and me. So we agreed to go in together in the nude, and as we sat there for a while, in walks Bob, also in the nude to join us. Zoe was embarrassed and tried to cover up, and Bob said there was no need to be shy and that we needed towels as well to sit in the saunas and suggested I go and fetch Zoe and me some towels, so I ran up the stairs to our hotel room as fast as I could, grabbed up two towels and flew back downstairs with the towels for Zoe to cover up with and said, 'Are you OK' to Zoe. She said yes, and then I worriedly and suspiciously asked her, 'Why is your face looking all flushed up and red?' 'Because it's bloody hot in here, and I am in a sauna if you've noticed.' My suspicions were all for nothing and very stupid of me as Bob was like a father to us, so I quickly got over that.

Another time on our second visit to Baden Baden to visit Maggie and Bob, we got on a train from Frankfurt, and whilst on the way to Maggie and Bob, we discovered we were on the wrong train, which was heading to Basil in Switzerland, and then at the next stop at Freiburg, we asked if we were on the right train to Baden Baden and was told we were on the wrong train, so whilst Zoe who got out of the train to ask the German guard for info, he said to her, 'Shnell, shnell', meant hurry up, the train cannot wait too long at this stop. Meanwhile, I was still on the train with our luggage, and the train was starting to pull away, and Zoe was still on the platform and was trying to tell the guard that I was still on the train, but he didn't understand her English, so Zoe desperately ran along with the moving train and yanked open the carriage door, and in doing so, the train immediately came to a halt.

I immediately started to get out very worried and nervously shouted out to the guards with my hands up in the air, 'Don't shoot!' The guards looked at Zoe and me and shook their heads as if they were saying, 'Crazy people.' If I hadn't have got off that train, the next stop was Basil, Switzerland, with no passport, no money, no telephone contacts as Zoe had it all in her handbag, and if I had to land in Switzerland, they might have thought I was stark raving bonkers, trying to explain to the Swiss authorities what had happened. They might have locked me up as some sort of crazy person without passport, money or any other form of identification. Man was I lucky that Zoe had saved me from disaster. We eventually contacted Maggie from Freiburg and told her what had happened, and she said, 'What are you doing in Freiburg?' Long story, we told her when we eventually met in Baden Baden, and she was happy to see us again and said, 'Maybe, Trevor, if you had to go to Switzerland, you'd be yodelling all the way back to Baden Baden.' Very funny, I murmured to myself.

Bob, who was like a father to us, treated us very well and didn't spare any expenses and wouldn't let us spend a penny, although we offered several times. He took us to all the top joints and fancy restaurants, including afternoon tea dancing in town, where the Germans did tea dancing. It was very different and a very enjoyable afternoon. Bob also used to get up at 5 a.m. every day to get us fresh-baked bread despite his health not being too good as he had some sort of blood disorder. He braved on and never complained, took us all over, especially when we visited one of their millionaire friends who had a fabulous Bavarian-styled house in the posh black forest area. She was a widowed rich elderly lady and treated us with champagne and the works. She took an immediate liking to me and was told I was a singer, so she asked me to sing, and I obliged. She was very pleased and suggested I come and stay next time on our next visit with my musicians with Zoe included as well. I was over the moon.

Bob and Maggie decided to come and visit us in England. We welcomed them with open arms, even went through the trouble to lay on a red carpet to welcome them to our humble abode at 23 Norman Avenue, where we had a four-poster bed. We gave them our bedroom and made them very comfortable as we could. Bob wanted us to take him and Maggie to the famous Harrods of London for shopping, and whilst at Harrods, Bob suggested that he wanted to buy Zoe and me a gift, which happened to be a chandelier, and asked us to pick one of our choice as Bob had noticed at our home that we had only a small chandelier and wanted to buy us a bigger and better one. We said, 'Please, Bob, we don't need it. It's too pricy at Harrods. We can take you elsewhere, where we could get it cheaper.' 'Nix, nix' was his reply and nodded to the sales girl to wrap up a large fabulous chandelier we had ever seen and still have it even to this day.

Old Bob was not keeping very well and was suffering from leukaemia and was getting top treatment for it but decided to go to Florida for a holiday and invited Zoe and me to join them in their posh rented villa for two weeks, which we did and had a fab time, especially meeting with their German/American friends, which was a special treat as we were taken by boat for the day to Sanibel, an island in Florida. We had a great time and got back only to have another party the next day to celebrate St Patrick's Day, which the Germans/ Americans take very seriously, all dressed in green for the occasion and danced exceedingly well, leaving me completely exhausted. I couldn't compete with them. They were real gentlemen in their manners and very politely asked for my permission to have the next dance with Zoe, who was lapping up all this attention, whilst I just sat there exhausted to the hilt, having a rest. All in all, it was a great event.

The following year was not looking very good for dear old Bob, and despite all the best treatments, he finally passed away. We visited his wife, Maggie, who was devastated and now had to sell up and move to a smaller flat. We met her sons – Klaus, Matthaus and Thomas – who treated us very well. Klaus was a super chef and treated us for the day at Heidelberg for an excellent dinner. Old Bob had decided with Maggie to leave us £2,000 in his will as he planned to visit us again in the UK but sadly never made it. We visited Maggie again the following year or two, and we noticed Maggie was not keeping too well as she was beginning to suffer with dementia and was getting worse. The years that followed, she was finally moved to a nursing home. Sadly and sorry to say, she now hardly knew who we were. We kept in touch with her sons, who kept us up to date, but sad to say, she had deteriorated rapidly and finally passed away too.

Rudy & Zoe

Michelle & Kim

Niki & Roger

Our 3 Blessed Kids left to right Niki, Rudy
and Michelle as they are today.

CHAPTER 23

MICHELLE (OUR FIRST DAUGHTER) AND KIM'S WEDDING, 1989 DECEMBER 8

What a wedding did it turn for our first child to get married and how excited we the proud parents were, especially myself, who was the father of the bride, and had the privilege to walk her down the aisle and give her away with tears in Zoe's and my eyes. It turned out a day to remember with me ending up completely sloshed and ended up asleep on the toilet in the new bride and groom's suite. Our second daughter, Nicky, and our firstborn son, Rudy, were there with Nicky, who was a bridesmaid, and a very happy but sad Zoe. We met Kim's (Michelle's husband) parents, Betty and John, who were now in our family and were a terrific couple. The wedding reception went off with a bang and, of course, with me doing my usual stuff with the 'Hawaiian Wedding Song' instead of a wedding speech, and everyone had a great time.

OUR FIRSTBORN SON, RUDY, AND FIRST GRANDSON, KYLE

The following year was another surprise with our son, Rudy, and his wife Zoe's wedding, and wow, what a wedding that was too. Rudy, our professor as we called him as he was the brainy one, was always advising me in all sorts of areas and was like an elder brother to me most of the time. His wife, who was also named Zoe, was a pretty and cute girl whom Rudy adored and very soon after surprised us of our very first grandson who was to be born, named Kyle, on 6 April 1989. Man, Zoe and I were so excited now we were grandparents with grandson number 1.

Our Second Daughter, Nicky, and Roger's Wedding

Now for another shocker in the same year, our second daughter, Nicky, and her boyfriend, Roger Campbell, went on holiday to Goa and gave us the biggest surprise that they wanted to get married whilst in Goa. Zoe went berserk, and so did I. How dare they marry without my consent, but they married anyway in Goa and promised to do it again in the UK properly?

When she told us the day of their return at Gatwick Airport, we thought we'd surprise them as well. As they came out of the departure lounge, we had arranged with the airport security to greet them with confetti as they came out, and as we did, the whole crowd of other awaiting people all gave Nicky and blushing Roger a huge round of applause amid cheers and whistles. They then did the official ceremony in February. Wow, what a wedding that was. I had to give away my second daughter, Nicky, the rebel as I called her. She was a biker, a hairdresser and completely different from her sister, Michelle, who was quite posh in her ways. Compared with Nicky, who was into punk styles with weirdo hairstyles and fashion, Michelle was into posh 'Burberrys' and posh friends.

Australian Tour

We lay low for a few years with me working on our house until 1992. Zoe and I with another couple, also Anglo Indians, decided to go to Australia as we had a special offer in the *Daily Mail* newspaper, where they offered a two-for-the-price-of-one trip to anywhere in the world, so we decided on Australia, which we did. We started with Perth, down to Melbourne, Sydney, Cairns, Alice Springs, Ayres Rock and finally, Dunk Island on the Great Barrier Reef. Man, what an experience that turned out to be.

Dunk Island was like paradise with massive large blue butterflies I've never seen in my life and custard apples as big as melons. Zoe and I had our second, third and fourth honeymoon whilst there. We'll never forget. Whilst we were in Melbourne at the famous Victoria market, we met our neighbours, Mervin and Beryl, who were also on this Australian trip with us, and whilst at Victoria market, we encountered these massive custard apples. They were so delicious that I bought a whole tray of a dozen custard apples, and Mervin and Beryl thought I was mad, but I bought it anyway but had to eat them soon as we were flying off to Bangkok in the next day or two. Man, did I get sick on custard apples.

Bangkok was known as the city of angels, far from angels, more like devils. On our first day out to visit the city, we were confronted with a smiling rickshaw driver. 'Do you want to see fucking, sir?' he said with a smile still on his face. Well, we were shocked but laughed it off and took the rickshaw anyway.

All these wonderful trips to far-off places I should be so lucky to have such a wonderful wife who arranged and took care of all the finances as she is such a wizard at figures as I am totally hopeless with figures and the travel documents, insurance, etc. This all happened whilst still at 23 Norman Avenue. Zoe's mum (the big bad wolf as I called her) was staying with us and keeping an eye on our youngest daughter, Nicky, whilst we were away in Bangkok and Australia.

MIRACLE NUMBER 1

From around 1992 till 1994 at Norman Avenue, I was getting itchy feet and decided to sell up and move to a smaller place as this four-bedroom house was far too big for us. I was fed up with commuters parking across my drive and having trouble getting my car out, so we decided to put our house up for sale. For two years, we had no luck with the sale. Zoe was at work, and I, the house husband, did all the necessary decor and maintenance to improve the house for the sale. Until late 1994, around June/July, our luck began to change, when one day we decided to make a novena to our Lord Jesus for nine days to help us with the sale and guide us to whatever he thought was best for us. Lo and behold, on exactly the ninth day of the end of the novena was a MIRACLE starting to unfold. I got a call and an offer for the sale of Norman Avenue. Now I started to look for my dream bungalow.

Zoe was at work, and I did all the running around with estate agents and harassed them to death to find me what I was looking for. The agents were getting fed up with my persistence and eventually found me a bungalow in Purley, Surrey, at Brancaster Lane, fully detached and what I thought was perfect, and so did Zoe. I now had my heart set on this bungalow and was making plans for the completion and exchange of contracts. Then suddenly, I was struck with lightning with the bad news that we'd lost the sale as another buyer beat us to it. I was devastated and nearly got run over by a car as I left the estate agents in a daze and sort of shell-shocked. Now the estate agent couldn't stop apologising and knew I was really upset and said he'd do his best to find us something else until the . . .

Our Miracle Home with terrace, 3 steps to Heaven.

Our beautiful garden view from our balcony overlooks
Purley Downs Golf course and super views of Croydon
and London, we've lived here since 1994.

Chapter 24

Day of Reckoning Finally Arrived
for Miracle Number 2

Whilst Zoe was at work, the estate agent rang me and said he had found me a place and thought it was just up my street according to all the specifications I asked for. He wanted me to meet him outside this particular place and would let me view the property, so I did immediately and met him outside this place in Purley, not very far off from Norman Avenue, and when I got there, I was a bit disappointed as I wanted a bungalow away from the hustle and bustle as it was with Norman Avenue. From the outside the bungalow, it looked a bit too small as I wanted a place a little bigger. The agent said that the bungalow looked a bit small from the outside and was a bit deceiving, so he said, 'Let's take a look inside anyway', and started to open the front door, and as we entered the hallway, which was wide enough but a little bit dark as it was early evening round about five thirty, he turned on the lights, and the hallway lit up. I thought that was better. The agent said the bungalow has a balcony.

Balcony, I thought, *not a lot of places have balconies in England as far as I am concerned*. The agent said he'll draw the curtains in the front lounge as it was a bit dark, and as he did this, lo and behold, my MIRACLE bungalow had come to life. I had to hold my breath and tried not to show too much excitement. The agent said, 'Nice view, isn't it? You can see the whole of the Purley Downs Golf Course, and if you'd like to step outside onto the balcony, you'd get even a better view.' Man oh man and cats alive, wow. Was this a super view, or what? It was like a film star's home. The view alone was enough for me. You could see as far off as London's Canary Wharf and all over Croydon. I felt like I was a king looking over his domain and all his subjects looking up to me. The agent then said, 'You can have a look at the garden below later on as it was getting a bit late.' And he wanted to show me quickly the rest of the bungalow inside, which he did.

We browsed round the kitchen area and the two bedrooms, which were so big it was even bigger than my lounge at Norman Avenue. He then quickly showed me the bathroom, which again was a bit like a film star's with gold taps fittings and an oval-shaped bathtub, shower cubicle. Gold taps, matching washbasin and toilet. The balcony measured thirty-five feet long and five feet wide. He then led me again to the front room lounge, which I did not see too well in the excitement at first, and when I saw it a second time, I thought, wow, wow, wow, the size was incredibly big and asked the agent what the size was. He said about 20 x 20 feet approximately and that we had to hurry along now as it was getting late, and he had to go and shut up shop, that I could come back the next day with my wife to view it again properly, so we parted happily with me still in a trance and had to pinch myself to see if this was just a dream, or what?

The next day, I arranged to meet Zoe after work for her to see this property, and as it happened, a younger estate agent met us this time and was a very keen and a bright-looking chap, who showed us around very well. Zoe told me earlier not to show too much excitement as she wanted to deal with the guy her way so as to knock down the price of the property. She saw the kitchen area and noticed the decor and kitchen cabinets, cooker, oven, etc., a bit outdated and required about £10,000 work to be spent there.

The agent agreed with her and told us it was an executive sale, and the owners were prepared to reduce. The asking price was £110,000, and we asked to reduce it by £10,000.

This agent, who kinda took a shine to us, said that he shouldn't be telling us this as he knew the owners would reduce to £106,000. Zoe then said to leave it to us to think about it overnight. The agent agreed and said he would put our offer to the owners and to contact him the next day. When we got home, I was really upset with Zoe as I thought she was asking for a ridiculous reduction and that we would lose the deal as it was indeed an incredibly low price. God was it lovely and how badly I wanted it I couldn't sleep that night until the next day to hear the good news.

The next day, the agent this time was the boss and said the owners have somehow decided to accept our offer of £106,000 and wanted to meet us. He was very surprised at this low price and suspected his younger assistant had something to do with the low price sale. Of course, he was at a loss of commission but could do anything about it; he was upset with his young agent for disclosing the asking price, so much so he transferred him to a different branch. When we asked to thank the young lad with a bottle of whisky for his help. We were told he was moved to another branch.

The owners of the property wanted to know whose hands the property was going into. As it happened, the owners' parents both had passed away and wanted us to look after the bungalow with tender love and care, especially the roses in the front garden, which her mother had planted and looked after. We promised her we would and parted on more than friendly terms. Her husband, also named Trevor, said he'd come and sort the boiler and other minor details around the bungalow. Man was I ecstatic I wanted to scream; I still thought I was dreaming, even till today.

My dream started to unravel the next couple of days as it hadn't sunk in as yet. I got down on my knees and thanked the Lord Jesus for answering my prayers and especially the sale of our Norman Avenue. After the novena of nine days and now this?

My Lord, I asked you to find us a nice place. I didn't know all the while you would give me 'PARADISE ON EARTH'. I sobbed and prayed and thanked the Lord from the bottom of my heart and continue to thank him every single day and will do so till the end of my days on Earth.

From that day that we finally moved to 79a Riddlesdown Road, Purley, I became a changed man, and my faith in Jesus got stronger day by day. I couldn't believe our luck in finding paradise on Earth and living a dream. We started immediately to get stuck in and moved all our stuff from Norman Avenue, garden statues, the lot. We started with the kitchen first, to renovate all of it, so we had a friend who helped us to completely refit the kitchen with new cabinets, cooker, oven, fridge/freezer and floor tiles and install gas and rewire the electrics, etc., at a price of £15,000. We were happy with it. It has done us proud from 1994 till today.

Zoe was still at work, and I was a full-time house husband, taking her to and from work every day, although she could drive, but I needed the car to transport myself about. We were having our kitchen retiled and had a guy in to do the tiling, and his name was Mick. Whilst he was busy working on our tiles, I had a phone call, which happened to be Mick's wife, and she said to me on the phone, 'Could I speak to Mick?' I said, 'Who?' She said, 'Mick the tiler.' I replied, 'Speaking.' She then said, 'You don't sound like my Mick', and then only did I realise what she wanted. I thought she asked for Mr Taylor, which I mistook for 'Mick the tiler'. My ears getting me into trouble again! I told Zoe when she got home, and she also saw the funny side of my day with 'Mick the tiler'.

Kyloo and Jordoo, two grandsons from my son Rudy.

Jordan (Jordoo) grandson no:2 and Emma
(Emmu) getting married in May2019.

My first grand daughter Tegan (Teagoo) and
boyfriend George as they are today.

My youngest grandson Ryan (Ryanoo) and mum Michoo
in background, he studies at Southhampton Uni.

My Magnificiant Seven. Front row l/R Tegan, Jordan,
Rudy, Max, Scott, Jake, Kyle & Ryan.

SCOTT SINGLETON (SCOTOO AS I CALLED HIM) OUR SECOND GRANDSON, BORN 24 DECEMBER 1994 THE START OF THE MAGNIFICENT SEVEN (GRANDKIDS)

Before we left Norman Avenue, Michelle (our first daughter) and her husband, Kim, had their first son, Scotoo. He was a treat from the day he was born, such a cutie. We loved him from day 1, and of course, we were landed as babysitters as well. Me being retired and at home as a house husband, I coped with him very well. Plus, Michelle was busy, with taking over the hairdressing business from Nicky, who owned it whilst we lived in Norman Avenue.

Nicky ran it very successfully, although she was just 19 years of age for a few years, but then decided to sell it to Michelle, so Michelle had her hands full, whilst I looked after Scotoo, and Zoe was at work. I used to have fun with Scotoo whilst he was growing up fast, and when he was about 2 or 3 years, I used to play with him. At the same time, I was more relaxed with him at the time. I was able to cope with him as compared with when we had our own three kids. I wasn't mature as I am now. Scotoo used to help me a little as he liked getting involved with planting spring bulbs in my garden and lots of bits and bobs around the house. I had a fishpond at the end of my garden, and Scott and me used to feed my goldfish. He also helped me when I used to roll my cigarettes and used to imitate my Anglo Indian way when I used to say things like 'roll it, lick it'. I used to drag the word 'roll it and lick it!' It was funny as Scott had an English way of saying words and not quite an Anglo Indian way. I said different words in my AI accent.

Scotoo now had a brother five years later named Ryan. I called him Ryanoo, a real cutie of a boy whom I also looked after whilst his mother, Michelle, went to work. Then one day, when Ryanoo was at play in my back garden, I decided to let him feed my goldfish at my pond. He wore my baseball cap, which was a bit big for him. He couldn't see very well where he was treading, and whilst feeding my fish, he tripped and fell into my pond headfirst. I was in complete shock but had the quick response to grab hold of his anorak and hauled him out and into my arms. He was white as a sheet, and I was beginning to panic but ran as fast as I could indoors. Zoe was there to help me out and quickly revived good ol' Ryanoo and quickly cleaned him up and ran him a hot bath and changed his wet clothes for my T-shirt, cleaned and powdered him up, before his mother came to pick him up. 'Why is he looking so clean and fresh, and why is he wearing dad's T-shirt?' We couldn't find an answer for her.

Scotoo and Ryanoo spent an awful lot of time at our place as I was always babysitting for them but loved every minute of it. Zoe was at work so much so that when she'd come home for lunch sometimes whilst I was babysitting, Scott or Ryan would answer the door and say to Grandma Zoe, 'What are you doing here?' and she would say, 'Excuse me, but I do live here.' Wow, I had so much fun with those two lovely boys.

My first grandson, Kyle (my son Rudy's son), was also very fond of me as I spent quite some time with him as much as possible, but

Rudy and his wife, also Zoe, decided to move off to Wiltshire about two-hour drive away from us; thus, we didn't see Rudy, Zoe or Kyle very much for a while. Then Rudy and Zoe had a second son, Jordan (I called him Jordoo), and then a daughter, Tegan (I called her Tegoo), with Rudy and his wife, Zoe, all living so far away from us, whom we didn't see very often, as we did with Michelle's kids as she lived only half an hour away from us.

Scotoo and his girl friend Fenn (Fennoo) as they are today.

The magnificiant Seven at my 70th birthday, left to right, Kyle .Jordan,
Tegan, Max, Jake, Ryan and Scott, myself behind Ryan

Maxoo and his girlfriend Sabrina (Saboo)
as they are today

Second youngest grandson Jake (Jakoo)
and girl friend Anna (Annoo)

MY VERY FIRST KEYBOARD

Keyboards myself, Vince on guitar, Kenny Joseph
drums at Ledlie's party, Hove Sussex.

Steve Wilde was a guy who worked at a music shop in Croydon. I happened to pop in one day and looked around the shop. Steve came up to me and said if he could help me. I told him I was looking at the keyboards and probably interested. Steve showed me a few. I told Steve that I did not know how to play the piano or keyboards and would love to learn how to do so. He then said to me that if I was interested, he could give me lessons as it was quite easy to learn this sort of automated keyboard, and he could even come to my home and give me lessons, so I agreed a date for him to come over. He brought a second-hand Yamaha PSR 450, which I bought from him, as he gave me a demo at home, and I was quite pleased.

Steve then came over for my first lesson, and I was a bit slow in picking it up. Steve said that it would all happen gradually. I had basic knowledge of guitar chords, and Steve said that knowing guitar chords would be an immense help as I could play the guitar chords on the left side of the keyboards and would end up with automatic backing to various songs that I knew. With Steve telling me this, I was away with one of my favourite Elvis songs for a start. The keyboard being fitted with a microphone was a bonus, so I started with 'Love Me Tender', and as I sang the first few lines, Steve stood there with his mouth open and in shock as I was singing and said to me, 'Man, you sound like Elvis.' I told him that I did Elvis songs for nearly all my life. Steve was amazed with my singing. and the biggest surprise was that Steve. who was only 22 years old, then told me he was an Elvis fan and totally loved the man. We then got talking about Elvis, and I told him most of my background.

Steve was amazed and then said to me that he would like to play the keyboard whilst I sang. He got on the keyboards and started to play 'Love Letters Straight from the Heart'. He was playing it so beautifully that I couldn't help to grab hold of the mic and started singing it to his backing. Steve loved it and then said to me, 'Stick to the singing, Trev, and let me be your backing keyboard player.'

I laughed and said, 'Are you serious?' 'Sure as hell' was his reply. From that moment on, Steve and I became best buddies. I learnt a lot on my own and got more and more into this keyboard. I found that the backing was so good. It was like being backed by a whole band or an orchestra if you like. I was gradually getting more used to it and thought that I could become a one-man band. Why bother with all those musicians who didn't back me too well as I expected them to? As a one-man band, I would earn more money than as I did with four or five guys sharing the money.

Steve had a girl friend called Carla, who used to sing at an Italian restaurant, the La Lanterna, in Croydon; she used backing music on CDs, which I thought sounded very good. It was a new idea then, so I asked Steve how Carla got those backing tracks and what the costs were. He then said he'd take me to the place that sold them, so he and I went, and I bought a few discs of backing tracks of Elvis, which were quite expensive then, but I was quite happy with them.

What started me off was the fact that one evening when Steve took me to hear Carla singing at the La Lanterna, she was pretty good doing her Madonna songs until she took a break. Steve mentioned to her that I was a good Elvis singer, and Carla happened to have a CD with a couple of Elvis songs and if I would like to try them and do a couple of songs. I agreed and took to the stage the next moment with Steve turning on the backing disc and me ready on the stage with the mic.

I was raring to go, and as soon as the music started, I was gone man and gave it my best. The next thing I heard was a thunderous applause from the audience who shouted out for more. I was quite surprised how well it went down with the crowd, and so was the restaurant owner named Marco, so much so he approached me quickly and offered me a few bookings there with Carla sharing it with me as well.

Carla and I were happy to oblige, so we did a few gigs there until the end of that year, 1998, and whilst performing there, I was approached by one of the guys in the restaurant who handed me a £20 note and asked to see me after my act, which I did later on. This guy happened to be a very rich Indian, who wanted me to come and perform at his son's birthday on New Year's Eve and would pay me whatever I would charge. I then told him I was still at the La Lanterna and had to honour my contract for New Year's Eve. He said to me that it wasn't a problem, if I finished my gig at midnight to come over to him after that as his party was going on all night till the early hours of the morning, so I agreed and did as planned.

I then got to this guy's party just after midnight with all my speakers, amps and backing tracks, ready to do my Elvis thing, and to my surprise, the son whose birthday it was, was a true Elvis fan, and so were a few of his mates who all hired Elvis costumes and wigs. They all came to help me with my gear and helped me get set up. The party was in a huge marquee and very grand, with tons of booze and exotic Indian food. Man, what a night it turned out to be. It was a very happy start to a very happy new year 1999, so much so that the guy wanted me for his next new year to bring in the year 2000. He said he'd pay me whatever I wished for. I gave him a price. He didn't hesitate to agree as money was no problem for him. The sad news was come the year 2000, I was getting ready for this big bash, only to discover that this rich Indian was a bit of a Mafia dealer and was in prison for money laundering, and so I lost out big time because for a New Year gig, you get good money, but that's Sods Law!

Chin up, I said and carried on my friendship with Steve, who took me to his home to meet his mum and dad. I discovered that Steve was a classical pianist, and his parents were quite surprised that Steve was into Elvis, and I was this Anglo Indian Elvis, but they kinda liked me and made me very welcome and welcomed me to a house party for Steve's twenty-third birthday, which went off very well with Steve backing me on his keyboard and Steve's sister and family enjoying the show.

Now although Steve was an excellent pianist he was very shy to perform in front of an audience, and I tried to make him get over this, but he would not do it. When he saw an audience, he just froze. No matter what encouragement I gave him, he wouldn't budge, and that was that!

SHORT TRIP TO SRI LANKA, 1996

This trip was not planned but was sort of spur of the moment. Sri Lanka was very beautiful and so very green, a paradise on Earth. We stayed at a beach resort for a week. There was a local Sri Lanka band guys doing their stuff. One of the nights, I approached the band and asked to do a few numbers with them. The following night, whilst doing my stuff with the band guys, I decided to take the hat around for the poor workers of the Sri Lankan village. I collected quite a large sum of donations from the audience. The following day, I handed over all the cash I collected. I felt very proud to do this act of charity. Our short trip then ended on a good note. We flew back the following day.

My India Tour, 1998

Zoe and I both wanted to visit India again and made the plans to cover as much as we could in four weeks as that was all the leave Zoe could get from her work, so we planned it with another couple, Arthur and Marie, to visit Delhi; Agra, Zoe's birthplace; Nagpur, where I was born; Calcutta; Bombay and Kerala in South India.

We flew to Delhi and booked in at the YMCA for a few days, whilst I got to start my trip down memory lane, by going to Wenger's Restaurant, where I first started my singing with the Carl Mannet band and where I first met Zoe. I was very sad to learn that the restaurant was no more but only consisted of a patisserie down below. Then after a few enquiries, we found out the original boss's son was still around, and we managed to see him. He gave us the lowdown on how Wenger's was shut, and he remembered me from 1957/58, when I did my thing there and how I flung the mic from side to side during my performances and driving all the young girls crazy. We left there quite happily and took home a few of the famous Wenger's patties. Wow, were they delicious.

We strolled around Delhi's Connaught place and then took a rickshaw back to Arthur and Marie's hotel to finish off some lovely kebabs and those delicious patties. Arthur and Marie were preparing to go to Calcutta, and we were preparing our pre-booked trip to Agra, where Zoe was born, so we parted from Arthur and Marie and said we'd meet them again in Bombay.

Zoe and I had our pre-booked tickets in the UK for Agra on the train. Whilst heading for the station at 5 a.m. to get the 6 a.m. train, we were confronted by an Indian man who offered to help us locate our train. He said that we should follow him to his boss's office, who would help us with our journey to Agra. When we got to this office of his 'so-called boss', we discovered his boss was getting very stroppy with us, asking to see our passports and travel documents. We told him that we were pre-booked from the UK, and everything was paid for. He then started arguing with us that our tickets were no good in India, and we'd have to get new tickets from him. Then we really got mad with him as the time was ticking away for our 6 a.m. train. I started to tell this bloke who claimed to be the manager that we had enough of his attitude towards us. He said in a cocky manner that without his permission, we could go 'nowhere'.

I was furious by now and told this so-called manager that he was trying to con us, that we were born in this country and expected to be treated fairly and not conned. We were not just ordinary tourists; we were just visiting our place of birth and didn't expect to be cheated like this.

By now, Zoe's patience had come to an end. She just grabbed hold of our tickets he was holding in his hands, and seeing the anger in our eyes, he let go of our tickets. We hurried down to the station with this Indian guy following us and apologising for his boss's behaviour. He'd showed us our platform for our train. We were desperate by now as time was running out, and we finally saw our names on a list this guy should have shown us in the first place. I was boiling mad with rage and couldn't relax. I wanted to go back and sort out that bastard so-called manager. I sat on this train and wanted to go back and sort out this son of a bitch. How dare he try to cheat us? We were innocent visitors back to our country of birth. I wanted to go back and tear his heart out. Fuck the trip to Agra. I wanted revenge so bad I was shaking with anger until I noticed a very calm and soft-spoken Bengali man in front of me who tried to calm me down as he guessed what had happened to us and said that it was not worth getting upset and let that be a lesson to us that in India, there are many touts like this and to be very careful from now on and that if I wanted revenge, it would do me no good as these touts operate in gangs that I would only end up in prison by the very corrupt police, and once in prison, it would be very difficult to get out. I then calmed down and knew there was nothing I could do and was very sad that coming back to India was a disaster. Anyway, the train finally took off on its way to Agra.

Agra was a very dusty old town. Zoe had a cousin still living there, Gary Phillipowsky, who met us at the station and made us welcome at his home. He showed us Zoe's home where she was born, but she didn't want to enter it, seeing the state it was in. Gary took us to his home, and we met his family. Gary showed us his new home being built with marble and the finest of its kind as Agra was full of marble. His terrace was overlooking the famous Taj Mahal. Wow, all for a cost of £10,000. We tried visiting the Taj Mahal, but being a Monday, it was closed to visitors, and plus, it was a very misty day; we wouldn't get a proper view. After some lunch with Gary's family, we visited his brother Ivan, who was in the army and had a big posh house. We then went with Gary to an Indian sweets shop to buy some of the famous sweets of Agra. Man, were they fantastic.

We left Agra for a train journey to Calcutta, no problems this time as we arrived in the 'City of Joy' as it was called. Joy my ass; it looked like the pits, dirty, filthy, overcrowded streets and whatnot until we took a taxi to our pre-booked hotel, only to find it looking like a brothel. I refused to book in, with the manager of the hotel running after me saying that I'd booked this hotel and had to fulfil my booking. I turned round and told him to get lost very firmly, and he did. We then told the taxi guy to find us a decent hotel, and he did find us a nice, friendly hotel run by Anglo Indians, and a little Anglo worker from the hotel made us very welcome. Later on, he offered to take us to his humble home he had under a railroad track. It was so small and neat in the little space he had, but he was happy and then showed us round Calcutta's Newmarket area. We had some of Nizam's famous kebabs.

We then grabbed hold of a human-drawn rickshaw, which we had never been on before. We ended the short trip of our shopping back to our hotel. We made sure we tipped the rickshaw guy very handsomely; he looked up at the sky and thanked God. He then quickly tucked the money away before anyone could see him. I heard that Cal was famous for its nightclubs and went in search to listen to some live music, only to find some dingy places with a small band trying to sound like the Eagles and singing Hotel California not very well, so we left. Very disappointed with dirty and smelly old Cal, we left for Nagpur, where I was born.

Nagpur, city of the dammed, I called it, dirty, dusty and polluted. Shit, was this where I was born?

Never mind, I was here now and had to make the most of it. I cheered up when my cousin Lena Rocque and her hubby, Charles, met us at our hotel and was later on confronted with another cousin in the foyer, who kept looking at me. I said to her not knowing who she was, 'Can I help you?' She then suddenly said my name in a very sad voice and then told me she was Betty Moss, my cousin. I was ashamed of myself as she resembled my mum a bit; we then hugged each other and went up to our room for a celebration drink, with Lena, Charles and Betty.

Next move was to visit the house I was born in, which was my mother's house, 'the house of Jacob', the house of my mother's father', where I was brought up by my grandma and granddad, although I don't remember much as my parents moved to Bombay when I was about 2 or 3 years of age.

I met my cousins, the Francis family – Dominic and Barbara and their sons Trevor, Lionel and Leslie and Coralanne, their sister – and we all had a good old booze up with my singing and dancing and lovely food. Trevor my cousin took Zoe and me to visit my old school St Francis de Sales, where I was a boarder for the last two years of my school days. It brought back old and fond memories. Then I met the principal of the school, Fr. Laurie Fernandes, whom I'd completely forgotten, but he remembered me all right as he remembered how I used to sing and was a real pretty boy then and didn't care much for games, etc. Trevor, my cousin, then took me to visit one of my old school master, Sir Amaranth, who lived a few doors away from the school. I visited him and his two daughters. I later went to meet other cousins related to my mum, the Rocque family, Pat, Leo and Lena, and after all this visiting and very sentimental memories, my cousin Trevor and his wife sorted out our trip to Kerala, South India.

KERALA, SOUTH INDIA

After a two-night journey from Nagpur to Trivandrum on a train with very friendly Indian/Jain family we met, we arrived at Trivandrum and met by a friend of my cousin Trevor, a very kind lady dressed in a sari, who took us to her house and made us very welcome indeed, with lunch served out on a banana leaf and delicious curries, dhal, rice and very yummy indeed I nearly tore the banana leaf whilst eating desperately, eating and licking my fingers. Boy was it good, or what?

Next thing we knew, Zoe and I were fixed up to stay at this fab place overlooking the sea with a long stretch of beach and our own personal 'boy' to serve us with whatever were our needs. We just had to ring the bell, and he was there, morning, noon and night. He brought us fresh papayas, eggs, toasts, teas and coffees and delicious lunches of lovely fish curries and whatever else we needed. He was there, appearing like a genie. A few days of glorious sun and sand, we planned to move on to Kodi Kanal, one of the well-known hill stations of the south.

We were driven by an arranged taxi to the famous five-star Carlton Hotel at Kodi Kanal. Wow, what a joint, very colonial indeed with waiters in turbans and a posh reception manager, who happened to be a very well-spoken Anglo Indian, whom I incidentally met whilst in Delhi a few years ago. Tyron was his name, and he made us very welcome.

We then met some Indian holidaymakers who became good friends over that week. When we met at dinner, there was an Indian man playing keyboards and trying to entertain us with Indian and some English songs. He was very quiet and slightly nervous to play a bit louder, so one of the guests with us, who was a bit older, was sharing a bottle of whisky with our crowd as we were getting a bit merry. This guy, Chandra, with the whiskey suggested to give this keyboard player a drink too to make him a bit merrier, so we did.

Within minutes, the keyboards got louder, and so did his singing. We all got even merrier, and more drinks were flowing. All the other waiters gathered round to watch this tipsy keyboard guy belting away his songs as they had never heard before. Then to add to this razzmatazz, Chandra heard I was a singer too and suggested I sang along with this guy, so I did. Then all hell broke loose. The keyboard player let me play his keyboard and was soon singing along with me whether he knew my songs or not. At the end of the night, we were all well pissed. The next day, Chandra and the rest, a couple of honeymooners, all went out for a picnic. Great bunch they were. Chandra happened to be a doctor and was from Singapore. He gave me his card and invited me to visit him and his wife anytime we happened to visit Singapore. There ended our trip to Kodi Kanal and all parted happily.

Next stop was Bombay, good old Bombay. We stayed at the YMCA and met up with Arthur (who spoke very posh and loved his booze) and Marie, his wife. Now Bombay had dry days (no booze joints were open), so Arthur was not very happy. I decided to cheer up Arthur and took a taxi to Bandra in the hopes of getting some booze there. This taxi driver, who called every one of his customers uncle or auntie, and kept driving very fast. Arthur was getting a bit nervous and said to me in his posh voice, 'Damn it, Trevor, tell this taxi bloke to take it easy, old chap', so I did. Then the taxi guy said to Arthur, 'Sorry, Uncle.' 'Damn it, Trevor, tell this chap I am NOT his uncle and to jolly well slow down.' Arthur, by now, was really getting edgy and dying for some booze and getting more irritable. We eventually managed to get Arthur some moonshine and kept him happy for a while. Until we drove back to Bombay/Colaba, only to find no booze shops open.

The YMCA was quite comfortable, and the food was simple but clean and tasty. The manager/cook took a fancy to Zoe and kept offering her extra puris with her meal and didn't take a blind bit of notice of me, maybe because of my brown skin, which had got even darker. He thought I was not white as Zoe was, maybe. The rooms were average, but the air condition was diabolical and seemed to give out a funny smell of paraffin, and this was choking me to death. I was coughing and couldn't sleep all night. I thought I was going to die that night. I said my act of contrition and was ready to die but somehow managed to survive. The next morning, I was told they injected the air-condition system with an insecticide to keep away insects and cockroaches and was something similar to paraffin. Besides, not forgetting the pollution outside was diabolical. If you blew your nose, your handkerchief would be black as soot. I couldn't wait to get away from Bombay. How did I ever live there for 18 years in my youth?

CHAPTER 25

THE MILLENNIUM

We got back to the UK safe and sound and somewhere at the end of 1999, heading for the millennium, the year 2000.

Zoe then decided to go on a short trip to Turkey with our daughter Michelle, who by now had a second son, Ryan (I called him Rynanoo). I could not go as they had planned it last minute and wasn't enough time to include me, so I stayed at home and was quite happy for some space. Whilst they were away for the week, I decided to do some composing, my song for Zoe. I had got inspired being all alone and was able to concentrate on composing a very sentimental song.

MY SONG WRITING AND COMPOSING

I started with a tune in my head and then got down to writing the lyrics. I managed to compose a very good song for Zoe. 'Missing You' was the title; it was a surprise for her when she returned. Later on, I got inspired to write more songs and recorded them at my home recording studio with the help of a guitarist, Simon Eyres, who was a brilliant help with my recordings. My four songs are all on YouTube. I hope to be recognised as a songwriter someday.

Whilst Zoe was away, I phoned Kim (Michelle's husband), and I went to an Indian restaurant called the Panahar and was having a good meal. There was a bloke playing the sax and was quite good whilst we ate. Then when I saw this guy, who happened to be the manager of the restaurant, I handed him my card with phone details and asked if he was interested in engaging me as an entertainer. He took my card and said he'd let me know. Kim and I went home, and I thought no more about handing over my card. Then after a day or two, I got a call from the manager of the Panahar, who wanted to meet me and discuss hiring me, so I made an appointment and agreed to start the week after. In the meantime, Zoe had returned from Turkey with Michelle and her two boys, Scot and Ryan. I told Zoe about the song I'd written for her, and she was quite surprised, and then I gave her the news about the Panahar restaurant, and she was even more surprised.

Part Of Me

If I said I loved you and that you were part of me
If I said I miss you every single day
If I told you every day seems a lifetime
And that part of me isn't working half the time

Had I told you everyday seems so lonely
Seems like my sunshine's gone somewhere far away
Although my heart keeps on yearning for you dearly
And a part of me , Yes its dying each passing day

Chorus: Oh please come back to me you know you're part
of me
Well I just can't seem to function anymore
You and I were made to live with only one heart
And no power in the world can keep us apart

Yes dear your part of me has gone and my life has
no meaning
And my heart, it just can't keep away the tears
Seems like someone's come and taken away my
sunshine
Yes its raining in my heart girl, all the time
Yes you're of me, please come back to me , girl of
mine
Yes its raining in my heart girl, all the time
Oh please come back to me, girl of mine

Oh I never realised how much I really miss you
'Till you finally caught a plane yesterday
'Though you said it was just for a little while, and it wont be
long
And that is why I'm singing this song

Chorus:
So hurry on back to my empty arms again
Though my heart is aching for you every day
The pillow is still wet from last nights' tears
So I'll sing this song for you just once again.

Yes it's only been a day and my life seems so empty
Late night must have been the longest night of the year
Yea the king size bed, it's seemed so cold and empty
And the sweet smell of your body, was still there

Repeat Chorus:

Well I even tried listening to the radio
Every song seemed to be the saddest song you've heard
I even did some work in the garden without you
But the birds didn't seem to sing no more
As if they knew you and I were not together
And the wind seemed to whisper you name

Yea the big trees, they even bowed their heads in sadness
And the clouds, they seemed to bring down the rain.

Chorus (Twice) and fade away…

THE INDIAN RESTAURANTS

I started at the Panahar the next week with my keyboards and my
PA system, sat and started with a few tunes playing very gently, singing
quite softly as there were a few customers.

Then this manager guy came to me and asked me to turn the
music down, so I did, and after a while, he returned, whist I was
playing my music. He turned my speakers round towards me and
again asked me to turn it down. At this point, I was now really pissed

off and decided to stop altogether, turned my music off and went to my car outside and had a fag to cool down my temper.

Whilst in the car, I decided to ring Zoe and told her how pissed off I was with this job and was going to abandon this gig and just come home. Zoe managed to calm me down and convinced me to hang it out and return, try it one more time. After a while, I returned. As I got seated and started to play my music, a crowd of youngsters entered and were all a jolly lot, talking quite loudly. They were all celebrating a birthday. The manager then came to me and asked me to play 'Happy Birthday', so I did and then carried on playing but a bit softer than my usual. Then one of the birthday guys heard me singing an Elvis song and asked me to turn it up as he could not hear me, so I did. This crowd started getting merrier, and by now, the atmosphere had totally changed. The manager could see this and realised the party crowd was starting to enjoy themselves and started ordering more drinks and food. They got even merrier as the evening went on. I finally finished about 11 p.m., and the crowd wanted more, so I obliged with another fifteen minutes. Then I started to pack my gear and loaded my car, and whilst doing so, I was congratulated by members of the party on my entertainment and wanted to see me there again. I got paid by the manager and headed home quite pleased with myself, which was the start of my affair with Indian restaurants.

All Indian restaurants were like the Mafia. They helped one another and recommended me as top entertainer for their fat profits and therefore put me in touch with all their brothers, cousins, etc., who owned restaurants all over the place, from Croydon to West Hampstead, Gravesend, and the posh ones at London's Barbican area, where the clients were stockbrokers, from whom I got a lot of private bookings for private parties and paid very well indeed. I was really rolling in it. Bookings galore with my white-blue jumpsuits and black leather outfits. My radio mic and PA system, which cost me a tidy bit, was now being paid for. I was rocking like the 'King'.

Dubai

In the coming year of 2003, I was offered a booking in Dubai, where my cousin worked for Emirates. She told me she could fix me up at the Jumeirah Beach Hotel and get handsomely paid by the Arabs, so I decided to take up her offer. Then Zoe and I planned to make the trip to Dubai special, adding a holiday for us before going to Dubai, to spend a week in the Maldives. Wow, what a paradise island it was. We stayed in a water bungalow like two honeymooners, stepped out of our bungalow straight onto the ocean, which was crystal clear, and with exotic fish swimming all around you. Food and drinks were included; of course, the evening entertainment was provided by the local musicians who were very good and whom I couldn't resist to do a song or two with. Elvis was in the Maldives. I performed with them a couple of times, and me being brown-skinned like them, the other holidaymakers thought I was one of them and asked how I spoke such good English. One lady customer even offered me a booking in England and asked if I would accept it and travel to the UK. I then told her I was from the UK. Her jaw dropped in awe and said, 'Well, I never . . .'

I then moved on to Dubai and met my cousin Coralanne, who fixed me up a gig at the Jumeirah Beach Hotel, and it went off with a bang with filthy rich Indians feasting away on a huge spread of foods and weren't too interested in my act, so after a while, I got pissed off and cut my act short. Then I was approached by this fat Indian bloke who said to me, 'Why are you finishing so early? We were beginning to enjoy your show.' I was in no mood to carry on and said, 'The boss said I should finish by 11 p.m., and it was five minutes past eleven.' This Indian bloke said to me, 'I know the boss. He won't mind for you to carry on.' I said, 'I don't care who you are or how well you know the boss, but I'm done.' I just walked off with his mouth open in shock. I managed to enjoy the rest of Dubai with all those rich Arabs and left for home.

TREVOR THE GOSPEL SINGER

I returned back to the UK and visited my old Panahar, where I used to perform regularly, only to be told that they had hired another Elvis and said they thought I wasn't coming back. They thought I was offered a contract to sing in Dubai. By now, I was beginning to get pissed off with the Indian restaurants, although the money I earned was quite good, but I got fed up with the same old routine and thought I was wasting my talents on these useless joints until the day.

I met Fr Andrew Fernandes at St John the Baptist Church. He was a Goan priest, and we hit it off as we had a lot in common. I used to go to him for Bible classes with Zoe and started to tell Father Andrew that I did sing Elvis gospels and wondered if I could sing them at the church during the evening Masses. He said he would ask the parish priest for permission, so when I met Canon Jim Pannet, the parish priest, he said he'd give it a try and see what the results would be on his parishioners, and if anyone complained, I'd have to stop.

I agreed with him, and the next thing I knew, I was there that first Saturday evening with my keyboards and my mic, ready to do 'Peace in the Valley' during the communion time of the mass. I was a bit nervous and wondered how it would go down. I said a little prayer to Jesus and asked for his help, and the next thing, as my eyes were shut, I was surprised to see when I opened my eyes that some of the parishioners were swaying to my music on their way to communion. Canon Jim was surprised by the effect I had on his parishioners and said to me that I'd brought something new to his church and that I should carry on as long as I wished to, which I did for several months, and that was when I met . . .

David Palmer, who was the choirmaster and a brilliant musician. He heard of my Elvis gospels at the evening Masses and invited me to join his choir, but I had to refuse. I told David I would not be able to attend all the choir practices at the different Sunday Masses and was quite happy doing the evening Masses on Saturdays on my own. David agreed with me and said he'd help me with any musical tips if needed.

I snapped at this chance of this genius of a man offering me his time and was honoured.

David then turned up one fine day as arranged and helped me a lot with my keyboard and spent quite a bit of time with me doing 'Ave Maria' and other beautiful hymns. Then one fine day, there was a function at St Johns Church. There were lots of variety acts, and I agreed to take part. It was a very good evening with several good acts and then came my turn to do 'O Solo Mio' in Italian, which I had been coached with singing in Italian by an Italian priest, Father Ivan, from Roma. He grilled me for two hours with the correct Italian pronunciation. He taught me word for word with the proper Italian pronunciation until I got it absolutely right.

On the day I made sure I got it right, and then to my surprise, whilst doing my performance with my keyboard, David Palmer suddenly appeared and started backing me on the piano as well. He gave it that magic touch. I ended with a thunder of applause and thanked David.

The next act to follow was David Palmer himself who sat down at the piano and started to play a boogie, and wow, I thought it was really fantastic. David then announced he was going to play the same tune 'blindfolded' and, wait for it, with 'gloves on' as well. Man, I thought that was crazy, but David the genius did the whole boogie-woogie without a single flaw and ended with a tremendous applause. David was also behind writing a whole score for a play called 'The Son of Man' and performed it at the Fairfield Halls Croydon with the St John's Choir. It was excellent, David wrote several plays, and I was honoured that David managed to spend time with me and giving me so many tips.

I was getting now even closer to Jesus that I was singing the Elvis gospels such as 'Precious Lord', 'In My Father's House', 'Lead Me, Guide Me', 'The Old Rugged Cross' and many more. I was getting this closeness to God, sang them from my heart, and I got lots of praises from the parishioners, who said that they felt truly inspired with my singing, so I carried on for a few more months with Canon

Jim very happy with me. Until I started having more trouble with my hearing and was having more visits to St George's Hospital at Tooting. My hearing was deteriorating. I was having a lot of trouble to hear well enough and was forced to stop my Saturdays at the church. Canon Jim and Father Andrew were disappointed but understood my problem, so that was the end of that era.

MY BONE-ANCHORED HEARING AID

It was now the year 2005. I got an invitation from St George's Dr Selvaduria, a specialist in bone-anchored hearing aids. I was granted an operation to fit me up with an abutment made from titanium, which was embedded in my skull just behind my left ear, and after this abutment settled in after two months, I would then be fitted with a hearing aid called the processor, which had a tiny battery inside and, when turned on, would send the sound vibrations to my inner ear into the cochlea. The operation was quite simple after being kept overnight and was allowed home the next day.

The night before I was sent home, I had quite an experience at the hospital, when I was sent to the recovery room after the operation; I had this funny feeling whilst coming round from the sedation. I was quite groggy and happened to look at this blackboard at the side of me and in my groggy state started to see different names on the board written in chalk. I strained my eyes to get a better look to see if my name was on it and noticed it wasn't. Then I saw this figure of a black male nurse and called out to him and asked him if the names on the blackboard were of those who had just died.

Was I next to be written on the list of the dead ones? 'Am I dead?' I asked him. In his Jamaican accent, he replied, 'No, man, me thinks you are very much alive', and with that remark, I felt a bit better. Then after a while, I discovered it was very silent, and I couldn't hear a single sound. I hysterically called out to this black nurse again, and I said to him, 'Why is that I cannot hear a thing? I came in here to improve my hearing, and now I am worse, although with wearing my old hearing aid, I am worse off now than before I came in.' I was getting quite hysterical and started crying and asked if my wife, Zoe, could be contacted as she would then come in and sort this problem out. This black nurse said he'd contact my wife, which he did. He told my wife I was hysterical and couldn't hear a thing. My wife told him I was perfect before the op and couldn't understand what went wrong and that she'd be there as soon as possible.

She hurried along late at night to get three busses as she didn't want to drive and got there before I knew it. Before she arrived, the black nurse in the meantime called for one of the doctors and told him about my problems and that I couldn't hear anything at all. The doctor who arrived came to me quite calmly and asked what the problem was. I then told him that I was worse off than when I came in. Even with my old hearing aid, I couldn't hear a thing. He then calmly asked if I had my old hearing aid on. I replied yes. He then fiddled around with my hearing aid, and then suddenly, I was able to hear again. 'Wow, Doc, what did you do? I can suddenly hear again.' 'I just turned your hearing aid on again. It wasn't turned on' was the doc's reply. I couldn't stop thanking him enough. What a fool I felt as the doc just smiled at me and went away. The next thing I knew I was in my hospital bed in the wards, and Zoe was there worried as ever after the emergency call she got from the 'male nurse'. There I was smiling at her and eating a sandwich as if nothing was wrong. We hugged and kissed. My guardian angel had just visited me. We both thanked the Lord.

Two months after the titanium abutment was settled on my left side of my skull behind my left ear, to enable a BAHA (bone-anchored hearing aid) was fitted whereas it was clipped on with a snap-on, snap-off movement, enabling the sounds I was hearing directly to my cochlea inside my inner ear, I was ecstatic. Wow, I was in seventh heaven. I thanked my Lord and the hearing aid department and went off home.

The Golden Oriels whom I did a lot of gigs
with David and Denzil Bartel

Me Amigo Luiz from Post Office
in Croydon, now in L.A.

Our newly found friends and neighbours, Ian
and Phyllis also (sexy) Stewert

Our German relations, Gerhard and Evelin great
grand parents to little Lily Taylor.

CHAPTER 26

WORLD TOUR AROUND 2005

My wonder woman was at it again. My guardian angel Zoe was now arranging a world trip starting with Los Angeles to Bora Bora, Tahiti, and then onto New Zealand, visiting the North and South islands, Singapore, Penang, Lankawi, Kaula Lumpur and home. We had to do this in two months.

There was so much to take in that I didn't know if I was coming or going. I met my friend Luiz at LA and spent a day or two there. Bora Bora and Tahiti was very beautiful, but as I was not so well, I couldn't bear the heat and couldn't wait to go for our next destination.

To New Zealand, which was very pleasant and was met at Auckland airport by a friend, Charlie Jordan, who invited us to his bungalow at Witianga, which was a beautiful place. Charlie was a great friend and made us welcome from the start; sorry he's passed away now.

We both moved on to take our flight to Singapore, spent a few days there and met my friend Dr Chandra, whom we met during our trip to India, and he too made Zoe and I very welcome and treated us round his city and home and gave us a good time.

We then visited Penang, where we were met by my Malaysian friends Sunny Maung and his family, whom we met a year or two ago and made us very welcome too. They are all Elvis crazy in Penang, and I entertained them with my Elvis stuff and all the karaokes, dancing and lovely Malaysian foods. I ordered a few suits and had it made in twenty-four hours as well as some fancy shirts, etc.

Moved on to Lankawi, a fantastic island, and Bali, such beautiful islands on God's wonderful earth, like paradise. I must be the luckiest guy on this planet. We returned home safe and sound and very tired but relaxed and took some time to get over this dream holiday.

We had a year or two at home until 2007, we planned to visit Brazil. Wow, man, am I living a dream, or what? My wonder woman just doesn't know when to stop pleasing me, so off we flew to São Paulo into Rio de Janeiro, had a fab two weeks, been to a football match at the famous Maracanã Stadium and saw the famous Iguassu Falls and the coco cabana beach with Brazil's local boys playing footie on the beach and then spent a week in an island called Buzios, also another paradise. We loved the Brazilian people, warm and friendly. We bought a few famous yellow and green Brazil football T-shirts for the grandkids and myself and some of their famous guava cheese and returned home safe and sound.

THE ABC GANG

During late September on that year 2007, we had another week at Devon in England with a gang, fourteen of us, who were friends mainly from Brighton. They were the Ledlies (Sydney and his wife, Joyanti), Ken and Jenny Joseph, Jeff and Veronica Derrosaire, Wendy and Brian Beatty, Tony and Judy Barreto, Peter Delehoite and Zoe and me. We hired a fourteen-seater bus from a rental company called ABC, hence the name of our gang. Tony did most of the driving. We hired a holiday home with our own bar, which we stocked full with our booze, and man, we had one hell of a good time, eating, drinking and dancing. With my keyboards and our karaoke, we sang and danced endlessly. Wendy was in high spirits as usual with her high-pitched voice and dancing on the dining table, Brian, her hubby telling her off. Then it was my birthday, 5 October, and wow, they all gave me a birthday never to forget. Brian sadly passed away two years ago, and before that was Kenny, my best loved friend, who was a drummer in my band. His death was very sudden due to ill health, and I miss him so much it hurts. At Brighton, Hove, we all met very frequently at the Ledlies and had loads of parties with Kenny on drums, Vince on guitar, Rhaul (Joyanti's brother) and their mother, Indira. Then there was Shirley (Sydney Ledlie's sister), who fancied Vince. Syd and Joy had a beautiful daughter, Shephali, a very pretty girl who also passed away a few years ago, and ever since her death and Kenny and Brian's, all those lovely parties came to a sudden end.

Left /Right, Zoe, Jenny Jo, Veronica, Judy B and me.

Tony, Self and Jeff (Dare I Say) Derrosaire ABC gang.

My lovely drummer boy Kenny Jo very sadly
passed away, we miss him dearly.

ABC Girl gang, Joy, Veronica, Audrey, Judy Barreto and Zoe.

My secret Harem. Jenny Jo, Veronica and Audrey.

Canada and the Rocky Mountaineer

Where on earth have I not been had it not been for my wonder woman, Zoe? She booked the two of us on the Great Canadian Rocky Mountaineer. Wow!

It was the most exhilarating experience of my life; the train took us all along the most beautiful scenes I've ever seen. We stayed on the train three days with food and drinks, very posh. We had a short stay in Vancouver, Toronto and the icy glaziers and had a helicopter ride over Niagara Falls and another one for my birthday over the Canadian Rockies.

Whilst on our return journey on the train, I had an awful accident, which happened during dinner on the train. When we were enjoying a very good steak, I discovered my top three teeth came off and were stuck to the steak. I was dumbfounded and couldn't even tell anyone or even Zoe what had happened. I just dashed to the toilet as fast as I could and then got the shock of my life when I discovered for the first time that I had three top teeth that were stuck together during a dental treatment that I had years ago. I never realised the dentist had my three front teeth stuck together and didn't even tell me what he had done. Perhaps he did, and I didn't hear him!

There I was, in this toilet on a moving train and praying to God to help me. After dinner was almost finished, I sheepishly returned to our table and took Zoe away and asked to be excused, covering my mouth at the same time. She asked me what was wrong. I told her about my shocking experience with my teeth. She immediately sympathised with me and offered to help and do something about it.

She immediately contacted the courier in charge of our holiday, who was a very kind and understanding lady. She was shocked at my situation and suggested I use chewing gum to try and hold these three teeth together. I said, 'But I don't have enough teeth to chew the gum.' She laughed and said that maybe your wife could chew it for you. We all laughed at the idea, but then she suggested that all she had on her, that maybe it would help, if I took a chance with her 'false nails' adhesive but at my own risks. I didn't have another other choice but to accept her offer.

I took her nail glue, and off I went to the toilet in the moving train. There I was trying to steady myself with this tube of glue, with the train rocking from side to side, till I finally said a little prayer and asked my Lord to please help me with this situation. The next thing I knew I was suddenly calmed and managed to get the glue behind the set of three teeth and in a jiffy managed to push them onto my top gums, and 'bingo', they worked and stayed there.

Until I got out of the toilet and joined Zoe, who was seated and waiting for me. 'How did it go?' she asked. 'Very well, I think, but I don't know how long it will last, and the only other problem I have now is that my fingers are stuck together with some of the glue.' She said, 'Show me your fingers and let me see the problem.' The next thing I knew was that she, in a very quick action, pulled my stuck fingers apart. I had a bit of a shock but felt better for it. Our trip on the train was closing to an end, and I desperately wanted to see a proper dentist as I became the laughing-stock of our journey, but the glue stayed on as I was very lucky to reach home with my teeth still in place.

On arriving home we were welcomed with the sad news that my brother-in-law, Phillip Bourbon, had expired. His funeral was to take place soon as they had waited for our return from Canada, and guess what. They wanted me to sing at his funeral service with my dodgy teeth. I could not refuse as I quite liked the guy and agreed to sing a hymn or two, hoping my teeth would hold out and not come off as I was singing. I was so nervous doing this and once again prayed to my Lord to please help me. The next moment, a sudden calm came over me, and I managed to do the two hymns quite easily. My Lord has helped me again.

Glen and Silvie Rodricks at St. Chads.

Second Nature band with Randal and Bernie.

Vivian and Brian Chapman

Desmond (asleep) and Gene Furgerson.

Brain Chapman and Brian Bowman.

Bingo sessions in progress.

Listening for announcements.

Prizes for roll over jackpots, with Lauren, Robbie Pink
in pink shirt behind Lauren and Sandra Spencer.

Tony Barreto, Leader of the ABC gang.

CONCLUDING CHAPTER

My wife, Zoe, and I have discovered a new faith. We have been married now for fifty-five long years. Every day we thank our loving Saviour Jesus Christ. We thank him every day for all his help and heavenly blessings he has bestowed on us, how to love each other and our fellow neighbours. He has blessed us abundantly with our dream home and financial situations, where we rose from rags to riches, so to speak. From the Bombay gunda I was, he made me see the light and took me out of the horrible life in Bombay to the UK, where I married my beautiful wife, Zoe, on 16 December 1961, and had three beautiful children and seven grandkids.

Sorry to say my beloved mother passed away in 2010 on Christmas Day. Also before that was Zoe's mother, Mona (I used to call her the 'big bad wolf'), who was very fond of me really as we got on like a house on fire. On her dying bed, she gave me that little smile before passing away as if to say 'I will come and haunt you, you bugger', because I used to tell her whenever she was ill at our house that if she ever passed away at our house, she's not to come back and haunt me. I am scared stiff of ghosts. She used to tease me and say that she would. I did sing for Zoe's mum's funeral and my own mum's as well. It was a very hard thing to do, but I survived somehow.

Besides being looked after all my life by Zoe, in sickness and in health, for richer or poorer, she changed my whole life round with her clever brains, and inspired by God and the Blessed Virgin Mary, she lived the most unselfish life. It would make her happy to go without rather than me or her children have whatever was needed. Her clever brain made our financial situation so good that I never dreamt would happen. I must be the luckiest guy on this planet.

She has put up with my dodgy hearing all these years and never complained once; she made sure she was always there whenever I had hospital, doctors, and dental or bankers appointments. Because of my lack of hearing, she was always there as my second pair of ears in case I didn't hear whatever important things were discussed despite her serious rheumatoid condition, where she lost so much weight and carries on cheerfully as if nothing at all is wrong with her. She says her rosary every day without fail and always prays for friends and family to be well. She is a living SAINT!

To add to my luck, she is the best cook in the world. She excels in curries, where she didn't have a clue when we first married, not only curries the Anglo Indian way but in the authentic Indian way, so much so our friends are amazed and say that she's even better than the Indian restaurants. She also excels in Italian, Chinese, Spanish, Goan, Malaysian and a host of others. The secret is that when she cooks, she cooks with LOVE, and I got to say, I swear that I am the luckiest guy on this planet. My kids are all mad about her cooking and ask her for her secret recipes but not Zoe. She has no recipes as how can she explain the love that goes into whatever she is cooking. She works so hard around the house and is very proud of the home that God has given us. She is now a special minister of our church, and I am so lucky that God has given her to me. There is a SPECIAL place for her in heaven without a doubt!

Zoe and me have not been too good in our general health. Zoe has been on a course of regular treatments for a very rare case of rheumatoid arthritis and had lost a lot of weight over the past five or seven years, but she has fought her illness very bravely and refused to be beaten for the strong character that she is, with her deep faith in our Lord and especially in our Blessed Virgin Mary.

Although I am not as devout as her, I have my patron Saint Anthony as I was confirmed with Anthony as my confirmation name. Saint Anthony works wonders for me too as I am permanently losing things, and when I pray to him to help me find what I have lost, he never lets me down. I also have had an endless faith in our Lord Jesus Christ and in God the Father and the Holy Spirit. I feel God has always protected me ever since I was an altar and a choir boy. I never lost that closeness to God all through my bad times in the wicked city of Bombay. I always felt God's protection and saving me from many dangers. All through my rough days of bunking schools, stealing stuff, smoking dope and drinking booze, God was always there. I could feel his presence whenever I did wrong. During my altar boy days, I got very close and confided with the priests at St Xavier's Bombay, and the priests asked me if I considered giving myself up to God. That if I got a calling to become a priest, I think I did get a calling but ignored it, and that is why till today I have never lost that closeness to my Lord and never will. He knows every hair on my head, and I know he's always there for me. Whenever I am in trouble, I just have to say, 'Jesus help me', and the next moment, all my troubles have vanished.

My very clever Zoe, the wonder woman that she is, happens to be very good at maths and managed to buy shares, ISAS and Tessa's, and managed to make our money grow. To let us live comfortably, that I never lacked anything that I needed. Our bank balance and savings she built up over the years were incredibly comfortable. We could have anything anytime. We never had it so good. We were able to be generous enough to our kids and grandkids with generous amounts for each one's birthdays, and if they did well at their schools and then universities, etc., my wonder woman was a genius with money.

She is the kindest person to people who are sad or despised by others and is ever willing to cheer people up who are down, or if they are hungry, she would give that person the last bits of food we had, even if she didn't have enough left. She would rather not have the food herself than to make another person satisfied. Not only with food, but her personality is also so warm and friendly that she'd melt even the coldest person's heart, to make them smile and end up chatting away, in no time get to know that person as if she'd known them always, even though they just met. She's been my guardian angel, especially when my hearing condition turned so bad, that she is so patient with me over the years.

My hearing has gone from bad to worse that I am now fitted with a super-powered, bone-anchored hearing aid, which is Bluetooth and compatible with today's technology, and I am a bit more happier with it fitted to my left side. I am being promised another one for my right side and hope to God that happens before I finish this book. I have to take my hearing aid off at night before going to sleep, and then I am totally deaf. Zoe and I have to do with sign language. One squeeze means yes, two squeezes means no, and then before I can say anything at all, Zoe starts giving me two squeezes, and then I get the message and turn around and go off to sleep.

Sometimes my hearing is so bad that when Zoe says to me to pass her the phone and I ask why, she replies, 'Because it's ringing', but we just laugh it off as we both see the funny side of it, and now I realise I'm really 'the Deaf of Elvis'. I still manage with my deafness to sing now with difficulties at small venues and parties and do some recordings at my home recording studio. That keeps me happy. I record a lot of Elvis Gospels, which gives me a lot of soulful feelings and feel even closer to my Lord. I have made my own recording studio, and when I'm inspired, I record songs that are my favourites and start composing new ones too.

Zoe and I have come a long way compared with where we first met and married and had a wonderful son, Rudy, and two beautiful girls, Michelle and Nicky, and seven grandkids, who are all young men now and a beautiful granddaughter who is a very pretty 21-year young lady and wants to be a civil engineer. My eldest grandson, Kyle, is another brain box whose 27 and has married a brilliant young German girl, Nadine. Zoe and I have just been to their wedding in Germany recently. They both met at Oxford University and now live in Germany, and Kyle speaks and reads and writes fluent German. My son Rudy has another young son, Jordan, 25 year of age, a teacher and still single.

My beautiful daughter Michelle married an Englishman, Kim and have two sons, Scott, 23, still single and Ryan, 18, another brainbox and single. My youngest daughter, Nicky, married a Scotsman, Roger, who has a motorbike business, and Nicky is a teacher. They have two sons, Max, 21, and Jake, 18, both still single. Zoe and I are very happy with all our children and all seven grandkids whom God has blessed us with.

My beautiful Zoe has taken me besides seeing most of the world. I forgot to mention the holy pilgrimages we had been on – the Holy Land and walked along the Via Delarosa, the Holy grounds where Jesus walked and Bethlehem, where he was actually born – which sent shivers down my spine, and we also visited Lourdes at the Grotto of Our Blessed Virgin Mary and Medjugorje Yugoslavia, Our Lady of Fatima in Portugal and Our Lady of Knock in Ireland.

Zoe has two sisters: Audrey, who is a widow, has a son, Frank and two daughters, Jackie and Linda, whose lovely husband, Dave, a South African, passed away recently. Olga, Zoe's elder sister, married Eddie Chapman and had six kids. Gwen married to Dave Eadon with four sons. Olga's sons Rocky, Russell, Lisa who expired earlier on and Jeff all married with children.

A special thanks to Jeff Chapman, who inspired me to write this book and gave me the idea of the title *The Deaf of Elvis*. Olga has fourteen grandkids or more, and we've had a lot of good parties with Olga's and Audrey, who became a successful businesswoman and owns a string of properties, and then there is Joe, Zoe's brother, who's married to a Scots girl, Mary, and Joe is still doing music and gigs a lot till today.

We still have occasional gatherings at my friend the drummer Kenny Joseph, who suddenly died two years ago, and I miss his cheerful presence. Then there is Sydney Ledlie and his wife, Joyanti. Sydney has also inspired me to write my book, but we miss those who passed away, and we try to brave on and keep going.

As the Frank Sinatra song goes, 'I've lived a life that's full and travelled each and every highway and more, much more than this, I did it my way.'

Yes, indeed, I sure did it Elvis's way, from a teenager till now I am 76 years of age and had a terrific life from the days of old Bombay till my days and years in England and lived most of my life following my idol Elvis. God bless his soul. Elvis was and will always be the 'King' who is and will live forever for so many millions of Elvis fans the world has never known. Nobody or no other artiste or actors or singers like Frank Sinatra, Bing Crosby or Rudolph Valintino has never ever had so many millions of loyal supporters such as Elvis's home visits at his famous Graceland home at Memphis, Tennessee.

No other performers I've ever known to have a following such as Elvis has every year. He has faithful fans visiting his Graceland throughout the year. He has coach loads of fans visiting him that no other artiste has ever had. He was the most handsome man I've ever seen, perfect features, build and personality and charisma with a capital *C*, so cool in every way possible, with his Southern drawl and mannerism, was typical of a Southern gentleman, that almost half the world's population do Elvis impersonations such as myself and millions others. My advice to all Elvis tribute artists is try to be yourselves as copying Elvis all my life did not get me anywhere. There was and will always be only one Elvis Aaron Presley.

'There ain't no room around here for "ANOTHER" guitar man, son . . .'

'Don't criticize what you don't understand, son. You never walked in that man's shoes.'
                                        – *Elvis Aaron Presley (1935–1977)*

'Walk a Mile in My Shoes'

My first grandson Kyle & his German wife Nadine, Zoe and me.

Our First Great grand Daughter Lily
(Elizabeth Taylor) A Gift sent from Heaven.

Lily with great grad mother Zoe.

Our first great grand daughter Lily (Elizabeth Taylor)

"Trevor on Piano"

A SUMMARY

Trevor Taylor an Anglo Indian who was born in 1940 in Nagpur, India, writes an outstanding autobiography, on his early life in his home country and his immigration to the UK, where he built a completely new life for himself and his family.

What makes fascinating reading, is his description of an uncertain and deprived childhood growing up in Nagpur and Bombay where he experienced the seedy side of the city and recounts his meetings with pimps and prostitutes and gangsters with a corrupt police force, his life in the ghetto side of the docks on the waterfront which echoes the life as a young delinquent Marlon Brando in the movie.

Trevor's father an alcoholic provided very little emotional and financial support for the family, consequently experiencing very hard times. Much is owed to his mother who sustained the family on her own. He experienced the trauma of his sister dying when she was only 16 years old and this was followed by his father's demise.

Anyone who grew up in India, will recognise and feel nostalgia when they read the account of his boyhood days of kite flying and the fun activities like *gilli dandoo*.

Like most young people in India at the time, Trevor was fascinated by Elvis Presley. In fact it was almost an obsession. He lived and breathed the rock n roll star and was inspired to sing and play the guitar. Consequently, he formed his first rock n roll band called the Teenage Rockers. His group were in demand at various night club venues and even featured in some Bollywood films.

It was while singing and playing at a club that he met a girl that was his first real love, in fact he married her and that love has been an everlasting one.

Being of a very romantic and sentimental nature, Trevor talks very lovingly of his relationship with his wife Zoe and acknowledges the tremendous support she has given him. In his autobiography he also talks about his religious and personal beliefs and feels everything he owns is a blessing from God.

Unfortunately, he began to suffer from deafness in later life and is still in the process of adjusting and coping with such an impediment. It hindered his ambition to make a singing career and consequently has had to bear frustration and anxiety.

Trevor has a great gift for self deprecating humour and recounts a number of humorous episodes relating to his medical condition.

Sydney Ledlie

Lightning Source UK Ltd.
Milton Keynes UK
UKHW011831170620
365168UK00001B/47